SINGLE WOMEN IN ASSAMESE HINDU SOCIETY

SINGLE WOMEN IN ASSAMESE HINDU SOCIETY

JEUTI BAROOAH

Foreword by
Ananda C. Bhagabati

GYAN

GYAN PUBLISHING HOUSE
New Delhi-110002

Single Women in Assamese Hindu Society

ISBN: 81-212-0416-X

Reprinted in 2012 in India by
Gyan Publishing House
23, Main Ansari Road, Daryaganj,
New Delhi - 110002
Phones : 23282060, 23261060
Fax : (011) 23285914
E-mail : books@gyanbooks.com
Website: gyanbooks.com

Printed at: Chawla Offset Printers, Delhi

DEDICATED
TO THE DEPARTED SOUL
OF MY HUSBAND

ACKNOWLEDGEMENTS

At the very outset I express my sincere and deep sense of gratitude to Dr Annada Charan Bhagabati, Professor and Head, Department of Anthropology, Gauhati University, under whose guidance and supervision I carried out my doctoral research. I am deeply indebted to him for his encouragement, keen interest and help without which it would have been difficult for me to complet the work.

I am grateful to Sjt. J.N. Das, IAS (Rtd.), Ex-Vice-Chancellor of Dibrugarh University and Ex-Director of Law Research Institute, Gauhati High Court, who extended valuable advice and help in the course of my work.

I express my grateful thanks to Sjt. B.P. Saikia, Registrar (Admn.) and Secretary, Law Research Institute, Gawhati High Court, for his valuable help and co-operation.

I am thankful to the authorities of Dibrugarh University for kindly permitting me to pursue my research in its Department of Anthropology under the guidance of Professor A.C. Bhagabati, formely Head of the Department of Anthropology at Dibrugarh University. My thanks are due to Dr. K.C. Mahanta, Head, Department of Anthropology, Dibrugarh University, and to all other teachers in the Department for their constant encouragement and numerous acts to help and co-operation.

I express my deep sense of gratitude to Professor (Mrs) P.B. Das of Gauhati University for her constant encouragement. I also express my grateful thanks to Dr. I. Ali, Gauhati University, for his valuable help and suggestions in preparing the thesis.

The main substance of the thesis has been provided by all those single women who spared their time to narrate their life-stories honestly and frankly. To all of them, who I cannot acknowledge by name, I am deeply grateful. Without their warm co-operation this study would not have been possible.

My sincere thanks and indebtedness are due to Sarbashri Dr S.K. Baruah, Department of Census, Dr Anil Bharali, Dr Javed Ali, Dulan Bardoloi, M.Com., L.L.B., Udayan Hazarika, A.C.S. and Gauri Regon, A.C.S., for their invaluable help in various stages of my work.

I am grateful to Sri A.P. Swami for the pains he took in going through the manuscript. My sincere thanks are due to Smt. Jolly Bharali for her elegant typing of the manuscript and to Sri N.K. Choudhury for preparing the figures.

I owe a deep sense of gratitude to my brother-in-law Sjt. Bhuban Baruah, Department of Economics, Dibrugarh University, for his help and encouragement in completion of the work. I am deeply indebted to my mother for her unstinting support and encouragement during the period of my study. I must also place on record my deep appreciation of my young and only son Jyoti-Tapan for his willing and voluntary denial of motherly attention for months together and for actively helping me in many ways.

I would like to thankfully acknowledge the help received from the staff of M/s Das Photostat. I am specially thankful to Sri S.N. Barkataki for his careful typing of the thesis.

I have taken due care to prepare the manuscript as correctly as possible. Despite my best efforts, many errors are likely to remain. It goes without saying that I alone am responsible for all errors of ommission and commission.

Jeuti Barooah

CONTENTS

FOREWORD

This book is the outcome of the author's passionate commitment to a subject of investigation dear to her heart. Dr. Barooah had been in the pursuit of authentic information, within the accepted framework of objective social anthropological and soicological field research, through the better part of 1980s on the emerging position, problems and status of 'single women' in contemporary Assamese Hindu Society. I should know all this, for I happened to be her tutor when she prepared the material for her doctoral thesis which was accepted by Dibrugarh University in 1990. I remember quite vividly how on numerous occasions the author, as a field researcher, got involved in the various issues that she raises and discusses in the book taking an activist position and I had to argue her back on the role of a 'dispassionate' social researcher!

The book, resulting out of the thesis, presents singularly relevant information, a point of view and a model for social research that are of importance not merely to the Assam region but India as a whole. She deals with an important segment of women in India whose number is on the rise, here in Assam and elsewhere, and it is high time we understand their special problems of adaptation to the changing society and coping with the demands of life. As I see it, this case study of Assam should have relevance in understanding the life situations of single women elsewhere in India.

The women who for one reason on another never enter into wedlock; women who are widowed young or in the prime of their life with crushing responsibilities of surviving and often raising children on their own in an alien urban world; and the women who are estranged or divorced from their husbands together constitute the author's universe of 'single women'. While as single women they all share certain common problems and difficulties, each subcategory also has certain distinctive characteristics and problems of adaptation. All these aspects have been competently dealt with, with copious support of field data by the author. I find the author's style of narration and insertion of case material as illustration to a generalizations or observation absorbing. The book is a very readable account which leaves one a little disturbed and even a little provoked to take up a social activist position, like the author herself.

I leave it to the readers to explore for themselves these qualities of Dr. Barooah's work.

Professor and Director
Institute of Social Change and Development
Guwahati

Dr. Ananda C. Bhagabati

PART ONE

GENERAL

1

INTRODUCTION

The background

In India, the age-old traditions of the Hindus have determined a distinct status for the women. The status relates to the image of the woman — pious and devout, married away early in life, loyal and obedient to the husband and devoted to the service of the family and the rearing of the children. The *Smriti* authorities extensively quote the old doctrine of perpetual subjection of women and their life long tutelage under their male relatives at successive stages of their lives. Kapadia (1988 : 142), while discussing the classical notions of marriage age, refers to the Hindu concept in the following way : "Woman is not fit to be independent. At early stage in her life she should be under the dominion of someone, her father, her husband or son. The idea of marriage was the transference of the father's dominion over her in favour of her husband."

This aspect is also highlighted by Singh (1980 : 62) : "Because of the *dependency assumption*, i.e., that a woman is dependent on a man throughout her life (father, husband, son), data derived from household surveys frequently assume that a woman is only household head or primary earner if there is no adult male in the household. "In the Indian society, women are generally considered secondary earners, and therefore, their contribution to the household economy, even if substantial, is regarded as supplementary. Her traditional status is also visualized as one of subservience to menfolk who constitute the dominant segment of society.

In Assam too, a similar image obtains with regard to the traditional role and status of Hindu women. Even today elderly rural Assamese women are heard to say : "Formely I was under the control of my father, next I came to be ruled by my husband, and now it is the turn of my (grown up) son to rule over me."

Assamese society, by tradition, is a rural society. In demographic terms also it has been consistently rural and continues to be so[1]. It is characterised by powerful sentiments of kinship, locality, caste and community. Social relations in such society are remarkably firm and stable. In the traditional rural Assamese society, despite a subservient status, the Hindu women of various castes suffered less from social disabilities than her counterparts in some other regions of India. Nevertheless, lack of opportunities for education, coupled with marriage at an early age, acted as a barrier to their progress till a few decades ago.

During the last few decates following Independence, the social situation in Assam has altered significantly due to various forces of modernization. The resultant changes in society have also impinged on the conditions of life of the womenfolk. Urbanization implies greater opportunities for education and economic independence for the women. Both in the rural and in the urban areas of Assam, there is a rise in the level of literacy among the women[2].

It may be assumed that due to the impact of education, the tenor of Assamese society has become more liberal, less regid and less conforming to the traditional feminine ethos. Women are earning and the feminine segment as a whole is becoming more

---

[1] In 1971 the urban population of Assam was only 8.87% of the total population distributed over 72 towns and the single declared city of Guwahati. No census was undertaken in Assam in 1981.

[2] The rising literacy rate of female population during the decade 1961-1971, in Assam, is given below :

	Rural (%)	Urban (%)
1961	13.8	47.0
1971	16.5	50.9

independent. Nevertheless, the age-old attitudes and mores create many disadvantages for the present day womenfolk.

Though emancipation of the Indian women and solution of their problems have engaged the attention of social thinkers and reformers for a long time past, these are yet to be resolved satisfactorily. The problem is even more acute in Assam where serious thinking and action programmes are less evident than in other parts of India.

Related studies on women

There are a number of studies made by social scientists on the problems of women in contemporary India. A few such studies are discussed here :

A.S. Altekar, in his book *The position of women in Hindu civilization* (1959), has dealt with Indian women from the prehistoric times down to the present day. He deals with the general lines on which the various problems that confront Hindu women should be tackled in order to get a fairly satisfactory solution. The author reviews the long history to make a comparative estimate of the achievements and limitations of Hindu civilization regarding the women and her problems.

Indian women today by Khanna and Varghese (1978) is an effort to study Indian women in all their aspects. This authoritative study is based on one thousand case-studies of Indian women from different socio-economic levels and regions. In the social structure of modern India, where the woman of today stands, how much has she changed in the last three decades, what is her psychological attitude to change — these are some of the questions dealt with in the study.

In another study, *India's educated women,* Blumberg and Dwaraki (1980) presented their findings on the urban educated women of Bangalore. The authors have expressed their views that women who try to meet the traditional obligations of Indian wife and mother and also spend many hours away from home in paid employment are experiencing a 'role overload' or a 'double day'. They say that education and employment are the mechanisms which lead the women to larger freedom and greater equality.

Women in contemporary India and South Asia, edited by Alfred de Souza (1980) is a collection of empirical studies on the interaction between traditional images of women and their new roles in the changing society. It offers a fresh perspective on women and factors affecting their changing roles in the socio-cultural milieu.

Inderjeet Kaur (1983) has analysed her findings in *Status of Hindu women in India* to show how the Hindu women are still quite traditional in their outlook. Studying the changing value orientation of Hindu women of urban middle-class families in eastern U.P., the author opines that they have a highly selective attitudes towards tradition and modernity.

In addition to the above, *Towards Equality,* the Report of the Committee on the Status of women in India (1975); covers a wide perspective, including all the important aspects affecting the life of women.

There are some more studies that could be cited here, e.g., Hate (1969), Kapur (1970, 1974, 1978), Jain (1975), Mehta (1975), Devi (1982), Rao (1983), Kaushik (1985), Pothen (1987). Many of these works were published during the International Women's Year (U.N.O.) 1975 and after. These publications focus upon the diverse and emergent problems of women in the rapidly changing social and economic situations of our country. Such studies fill up a much needed gap in our knowledge as to what is happening in the sphere of women's status in contemporary India and their adjustment to the demands of modern life.

These studies, however, do not deal with the problems of single women as a specific category. The problems of Assamese single women have not been studied empirically by anyone. The problems of single women are in many ways unique. These have to be properly understood. Often neglected in life and neglected by society, they languish in a tragic corner in which light needs to be thrown. It is felt that there is a genuine need for studying the situation obtaining among this category of women.

The Problem

i. *The Scope* :

As elsewhere in the country, the social situation in Assam, too, has undergone significant changes in the decades following Independence due to various factors and forces. In broad terms, the change-inducing influences may be traced to diverse policies and programmes of Government and other agencies as well as to urban-industrial growth. The pace of change in Assam has been relatively slow in comparison with other parts of India. Yet, the regional society today is no longer a wholly kinship-based rural society guided by principles of caste, community and local organizations. In the urban areas joint family living is fading out and the nuclear family values have enhanced the position of women giving them greater freedom than ever before.

In the last decades, there has been an explosive growth of education even in the rural areas of Assam. Migration from rural areas to towns has increased in volume. For women, there is not merely a rise in the level of literacy and education but also an upward swing of the age of marriage (see Table 7).

In sum, the traditional stagnancy of the Assamese rural society and its cohesiveness have both been significantly undermined by the external factors and forces of change.

When the social situation is altered, it is but natural to expect that the role and status of women will also reflect the change. Thus, while lack of education and rigidity of social structure would not permit any widow, divorceè or unmarried women to exist as independent entities outside particular kingroups in the rural society, in the modern urban context it is not unusual for such a category to emerge. This is because urbanized women are increasingly coming out of the orbits of the tradition-ridden families. In the urban milieu, education, delayed marriage and occupational opportunities, all of which reflect social change, pave the way for the emergence of 'single woman' as a definable component of the women's world.

It is important to mention that in the last few years, single women, as a discrete and important category has been perceived and identified by even the popular press. For instance, a Bengal fortnightly, called *Sananda* (specially meant for women readership) published a cover article in its 10th September issue of 1987, entitled, *Ekok Nari* (literally, 'single woman'). In this too, single woman has been defined to cover the three categories, namely, widow, divorcee and unmarried.

The reseacher has chosen this section of the Assamese women for the following reasons : Married women who form part and parcel of a stable social unit, such as a family or a kingroup, do not have to seek special avenues of adjustment and orientation on individual terms. On the other hand, single women are confronted with problems which are new to Assamese womenfolk. These problems relate to new roles, new types of status adjustment and acceptance of as well as integration in a changing society. For example, an unmarried woman has one type of role in the traditional joint family in a rural community but a different one in the urban setting, particularly when she is an educated woman. Higher education may have the effect of limiting marital choice for a woman since it is considered imperative that the husband should have at least equal, and preferably higher education than his wife.

The life of a young widow with or without dependent children has also many emergent problems. It was one type of role in the traditional Hindu society, but it has become quite different in the emergent urban milieu. Likewise, the category of divorced single women is a product of the emergent social order. These single women who were born during the last thirty years or so, have greater potentiality for realising their aspirations when compared with the women of earlier generation. They constitute a segment which has been trying to achieve adjustment to the demands of changing socio-economic and cultural circumstances on individual terms.

ii. *Objectives of the study* :

An attempt has been made here to study and analyse the social situation obtaining among a cross-section of single women. The object of the study is to ascertain the emerging status of single women and to examine how far they have been integrated in the modern Assamese society and what are the unique elements and problems of each category of single women. To be more specific, what sort of change has come about in the life of single women in the new social context? In what way have they resolved their economic problems? What is their role and performance as working women? What are the character and extent of change in their informal social relations? What are the quality and method of adjustment to overcome their diverse problems? What is the pattern of acceptance of single women in the social milieu? Where do today's single women stand in the structure of modern Assamese Hindu society? These are the aspects examined by the researcher. Another object of this study is to make a close examination of the current social legislations in respect of such women. Enacted legislations are out of reach of a common Assamese woman as she lacks the necessary awareness, opportunities and financial resources. The question as to how far the legislations have ensured their security in society or have helped them to improve their socio-economic condition is one of the main points examined in this study.

iii. *Hypotheses* :

1. Urbanization has produced, among other things, a two-fold impact on the womenfolk of Assam :

(a) It has provided new opportunities for education and employment to women, and,

(b) It has aided the break-up of the joint family system and the weakening of the kinship organization wherein lay the traditional security of women.

2. Consequential effects of the above-mentioned developments have not been the same for all segments of Assamese women. These impacts have contributed to the emergence of the new phenomenon of 'single women'. But while on the one hand, educational and occupational opportunities have provided enhanced economic independence to women, increased their decision-making power and enabled them to judge the traditional customs and behaviour—the break-up of the joint family and the weakening of the kinship organization, on the other hand, have undermined traditional social security available to women, especially single women. Thus while the former effect is beneficial, the latter is not, not at least till alternative security is provided by society to single women.

3. In attempting to adjust themselves to this conflicting situation, the single women have stepped into a somewhat diffuse transitional stage. On the one hand, they have been forced by circumstances to seize the newly opened opportunities for education and employment and, on the other, they have not yet been able to extricate themselves completely from the kinship traditions which still provide, though loosely, some sort of security to them.

Thus they constitute a separate category or 'class'. They have to create a social world of their own and seek friendship and understanding from other single women.

The transitional stage in which a section of Assamese women find themselves provides the framework for this study. The basic premise of the study is presented in a schematic manner in Fig. 1.

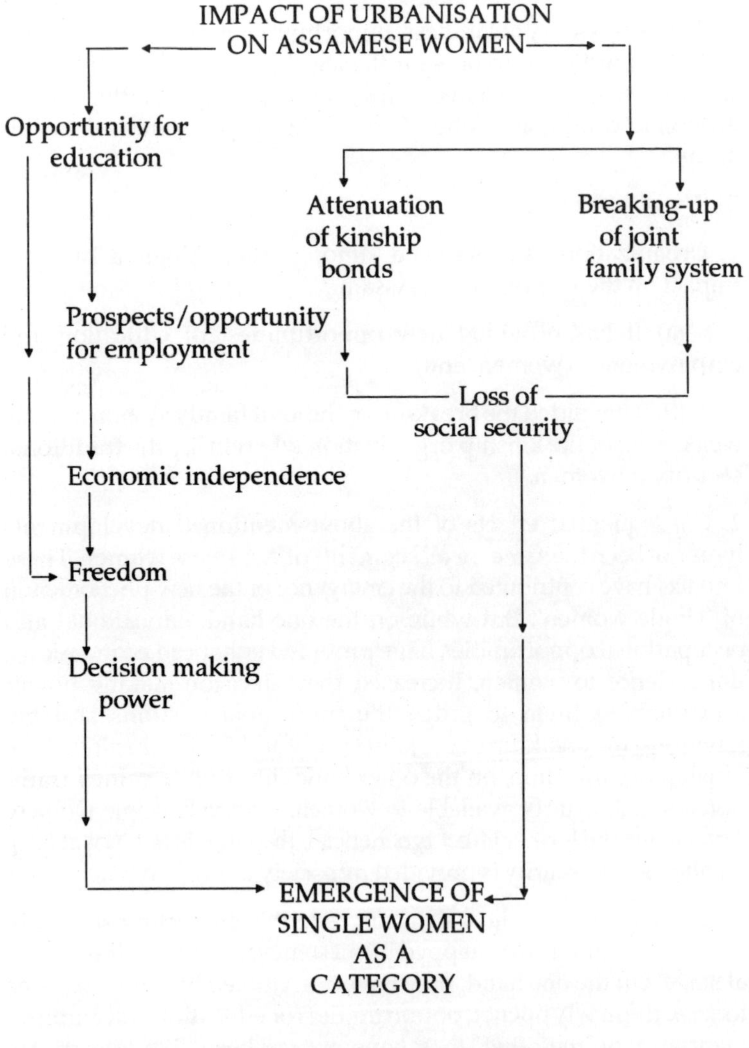

Fig. 1. The premise of the study.

iv. *The field setting and the universe of study* :

For a number of reasons elaborated in Chapter III, the new phenomenon of single women has made its appearance more markedly in Guwahati than in any other place of Assam. The researcher thus felt that Guwahati as a venue would offer more opportunities to study this new phenomenon than any other area. Hence the choice of Guwahati as a setting for field investigations.

The chosen topic of study, 'single women in contemporary Assamese Hindu Society', was originally intended to cover all classes of single women. But actual operational problems in the field made it imperative to confine it to that class of single women who were also working women. This is not to imply that all single women are working women. It is certain that there are many single women who are not employed in any gainful occupations.[3] But because of operational difficulties in the field they had to be excluded from the purview of the study.

Besides operational difficulties, there are also other reasons for confining the studying to the working section of the single women. For, it is work which provides the setting for consideration of the changing status, special problems of adjustment, arrangements for residence in unfamiliar surroundings, and so on.

Non-working single women are, by and large, a part and parcel of the traditional familial and kinship constellations. They are merged in the kinship system and, in the rural areas especially, subject to caste differences. In this study, though no direct and on-the-spot investigations have been made in the rural areas, yet data collected in the city from persons who have recently migrated from villages throw sufficient light on the problems faced by them in the villages.

In this study, the investigation has not been extended to the rural setting. Hence, there is no direct framework for comparison of rural and urban norms with regard to the status of single women.

Methodology

i. *Study design* :

It is necessary to mention that the study design is based on the assumption that single women are engaged in different types of economic activities. Keeping this basic consideration in mind, but having no secondary information to fall upon, a pilot survey was conducted at the initial stage in the various establishments of the city[4].

---

[3] A small number of such non-working women is represented by the inmates of Kasturba Ashram, State — Home and Destitute Home, who, however, belong to special categories.

Such establishments (as detailed in Appendix I) are of four different types :

1. Educational institutions, 2. Office establishments, 3. Banks and 4. Female occupational centres.

The educational institutions include Lower Primary schools, Middle English schools, High and Higher Secondary schools, College and University.

The office establishments include the offices of Central Government, State Government, Semi Government Institutions, Corporations and Boards.

Banks include the various branches of the State Bank of India and a few other banks located in the city.

Female occupational centres are those where service is rendered predominantly by females, such as, hospitals, nursing homes, weaving centres, hostels for working women and different welfare organisations for women.

The heads of such institutions were contracted personally as well as by correspondence by the researcher in order to have an idea of the universe of the single women engaged in these establishments. At first the purpose of the survey was explained clearly to the head of the organisation. He/she was then requested to fill up a schedule (Appendix II) giving names and information relating to the women employees. The completed schedules helped to identify the universe of study (as shown in Appendix I).

The result of this pilot survey shows that out of 125 different establishments, visited or otherwise contracted by the researcher,

---

[4]Names of such institutions were gathered from Telephone Directory, 1981; Administrative Directory No. 11 of the Government of Assam, and pay roll Register Books of the schools in the offices of D.I. and Inspector of Schools. In addition to this, discussions with various knowledgeable persons were held regarding institutions.*

*Personal knowledge of the researcher, who is a permanent resident of Guwahati, also facilitated the collection of names of such establishments. The list of such establishments where women, including single women, are employed in Guwahati is given in Appendix I.

as many as 105 had women employees. The pattern of female employment in these establishments will be evident from table 1.

Table 1
Women employees in the surveyed establishments in Guwahati

Type of establishment	*Total no. of establishment visited*	*Presence of women employee*	*Abence of women employee*
1. Educational institutions	35	32	3
2. Office establishment	60	46	14
3. Banks	14	11	3
4. Hospitals and other female occupational centres	16	16	-
	125	105	20

After processing the schedules of these 105 establishments, it was found that 10 schedules were not properly filled up. So these were rejected and 95 schedules, correct in all respects, were taken up for further consideration. The results of this pilot survey are shown in table 2.

Table 2 shows the distribution of population (1701) according to their marital status in each category of establishment.

In the first category, made up of educational institutions, it is found that the number of female employees is highest (38.7 per cent). It indicates that teaching is usually preferred by women.

In the second category, the percentage of women employees is found to be slightly lower (34.2 per cent). In Assam, women, working in offices is a new phenomenon occurring mainly after Independence.

Banks constitute the third category of establishments visited by the researcher. Service in banks is an new trend among the working women of Assam. Because of relatively higher salary, secured life, prestige and future prospect, educated women now try to get into banking services by appearing in competitive examinations. The percentage of women engaged in this sector is found to be 3.9 out of the total employees of 1701.

In the fourth and the last category of establishments, namely 'female occupational centres' (hospitals, nursing home, weaving centre, etc.), the percentage of women engaged is found to be 23.2.

Table 2

Distribution of women employees according to marital status

Types of establishment	*No. of establishment*	*Marital status of women employees*					*Percentage to total (1701)*
		Married	*Unmarried*	*Widow*	*Divorced/ separated*	*Total*	
Educational	30	523	90	32	14	659	38.7
Official establishment	42	343	184	47	8	582	34.2
Banking	10	23	37	6	-	66	3.9
Female occupational centres	13	98	238	34	24	394	23.2
	95	987	549	119	46	1701	100.0
Percentage of total (1701)		58.0	32.3	7.0	2.7		

Thus table 2 shows a good number (1701) of working women population in the 95 institutions. However, all of them are not single women. A high percentage (58 per cent) of these women is married. Then again, the entire category of the unmarried women who constitute 32.3 per cent of the total also cannot be treated as having the single women status. More than half of these unmarried women are below the age of 30 years.[5] Out of the total number (549) of unmarried women, 313 have not yet attained the age of 30 years. These unmarried young women have taken up jobs for various reasons. There is a tendency in them to marry at a higher age. It may be assumed that the unmarried young women below 30 years of age have the probability of marrige sooner or later. For the purpose of this study, therefore, women below 30 years have been excluded from the single women status as a measure of caution. In actual fact, however, a small percentage of them may remain unmarried and thus join the category of single women.

After deducting the number of married women and unmarried women below 30 years, the universe of the single women comes to contain 401 individuals. They constitute the focal universe of the investigation.

Table 3
Universe of the single women

Marital status	*Number*	*Percentage to total (401)*
Unmarried above 30 years	236	58.8
Widow	119	29.7
Divorced/ Separated	46	11.5
	401	100.0

Table 3 shows the break-up of this universe of 401 women according to marital status. Out of this universe of 401 single women, 236 (58.8 per cent) are unmarried women above 30 years. This figure also includes a few unwed mothers. Widows constitute

5 The age distribution of the wider universe made of 1701 working women of various marital status are outlined in Appendix III.

29.7 per cent of the focal universe. The somewhat smaller percentage (11.5) of divorced or separated women may partly be due to the fact that women of this category do not always want to disclose their status. The trend towards separation or divorce is a new phenomenon in the Assamese society and the women are found to be rather sensitive and reticent to admit this status.

ii. *Sample survey* :

After having arrived at the focal universe of 401 single women, the main sociographic study and qualitative data collection have been confined by 110 of these women. These 110 women represent a stratified sample representing the character of the focal universe in all respects. Stratificatioin was made according to marital status, distribution in various jobs and socio-economic class background. The study was intended to be intensive covering all aspects of the lives of the sampled single women.

Table 4

Sample sizes of single women according to marital status

Martital status	*Number*	*Sample studied*
Unmarried	236	40
Widow	119	40
Divorced/ Separated	46	30
	401	110

Table 4 shows the sample size of the focal universe. Of the 40 divorced/separated women as many as 30 (65.2 per cent) have been covered by the sample. The reason for including a higher proportion of women of this category is to study in greater depth the various causes leading to the dissolution of marriage and the manner of their adjustment to the demands of single life. Divorce or separation is a new phenomenon in the Assamese society and it deserves to be studied carefully in order to ascertain the causes and consequences of broken marriages. Hence, over and above these 30 cases 20 more cases were studied from the documentary evidence of the court registers, too.

The reason for taking a smaller sample of unmarried women is that even though they have all passed the age of 30 years, some of them may still get married at a later stage of life.

The proportion of widows in the sample is 33.6. This is considered large enough to give a true and representative picture of the actual situation.

The final sample of 110 women were interviewed in detail with structured schedules (Appendix IV). These schedules contain certain questions framed for the purpose of collecting basic sociographic data. But the interview was not limited to these questions only. All kinds of information bearing on the subject of study, besides answers to structured questions, were gathered during the interview duly recorded. Often enough valuable information were elicited from the women in the course of informal discussions.

iii. *Data base* :

The study is based on both primary and secondary data. Primary data were generated through questionnaire and structured schedule surveys, interviews and discussions with single women respondents. In addition, useful informations were gathered from a variety of persons, social workers, heads of various employment agencies, government officials, educationists, and so on. Secondary data consist of published and unpublished materials in the form of books, reports, journals and periodicals of historical, demographic and sociological nature. Women — specific studies were especially consulted to develop necessary insights and to provide comparative material.

Prolonged unstructures and informal interviews with single women in the sample enabled the collection of detailed cases. A schedule (Appendix II) was prepared in order to get sociographic and quantitative data on the universe. Two interview schedules (Appendix IV) were made for the respondents of the sample.

The study covers certain aspects which directly impinge upon the personal lives of the respondents. Hence, participant observation method was also used at times for acquiring as in-depth perception of the life and behaviour of the respondents. This would not have been possible through conventional and formal interviews.

Secondary data were collected almost entirely from the libraries of Guwahati city including the Guwahati University Library, Guwahati District Libarary, Central Library, Guwahati High Court Judges' Library, Cotton College Library, Library of the Census department and the Dibrugarh University Library.

iv. *Field work* :

It will have been evident by now that this study does not provide a conventional setting for anthropological field work. The single women, though a clearly definable category, do not constitute a community in spatial or any other sense of the term. There is no sense of identity or common sentiment uniting them as a group. Though the sample population lives in Guwahati, most of them do not know each other and they are not organized for common action as a group. All these 'negative' traits of the population under investigation made field work a somewhat unorthodox and difficult proposition for the researcher. Except for inmates of women's Homes, there was little scope or prolonged personal observation and informal contact and communication of the researcher with the women. Hence, with every single woman who furnished information, the researcher had to establish personal contact, rapport and communication links. With most of the informants, an interview situation was the first and sometimes the only method of data collection. From this point of view, the method of data collection was more sociological than anthropological.

Field work involved considerable movement to different parts of the city and getting involved in numerous interview type discussions with concerned women respondents. However, to the great satisfaction of the researcher. It was possible to win the confidence and friendship of many of these women, so that information came forth readily once they understood the academic and welfare orientation implicit in the study. The status of the researcher as a single woman herself, belonging to the same Hindu Assamese social universe, greatly helped in winning the confidence and friendship of the respondents as well as establishing the empathy, so necessary for probing into sensitive, personal and emotional arenas of life of the respondents.

The study necessitated collection of detailed case history of single women. But biographical details are always sensitive matters and could not be gathered in an off-hand manner in the very first meeting with a respondent. Therefore, in reality, an interview technique had to be developed during the course of the field work. Interviews could be successful when the purpose of interviewing the respondents was clearly explained. To gain authentic information it was explained to everyone of them that the researcher wanted to know the details of life of single women as a basis for general understanding of their problems of adjustment in society. It was also assured to them that the information disclosed to her would be kept strictly confidential and used only for research purpose without name and identification of the informant being made public. They helped the researcher honestly and sincerely by giving all the required information. Some women were highly articulate but others gave brief answers and appeared to be reticent. They did not like to reveal their personal life-history. Their hesitation was a great hurdle to the researcher. To overcome such difficulties, the researcher tried to make the interview situation as informal as possible. The quality of the interviews varied according to the temperament of the respondent. The questions were of the 'open-ended' variety and were asked in such a manner that they had to be answered in several sentences. Sometimes it took a minimum of two to three hours to complete an interview. Sometimes, depending upon the mood of the women, it required two or even three visits to complete the task. An effort was made to establish fruitful friendship and rapport between the particular respondent and the researcher. It was realised that the sincere and friendly visit of the researcher to their places was a great relief to some of the respondents.

The place of interview was fixed by according to the desire and convenience of the respondents and the presence of any third person was excluded as far as possible. The setting for interviews and discussions varied from home to hostel to a suitable corner of office where a respondent worked. Except for certain basic facts, no recording was done at the time of the interview. Note making in the course of an interview seemed to impede the flow of conversation and disturb the informal atmosphere. Immediately after the interview, every detail was noted down meticulously. All the answers regarding various aspects of her life were recorded as narrated by the respondents.

The field work for this study formally began in November, 1981 and was carried up to around 1985. The basic field data generation took place during the period of 1982-1983.

Tabulation and Interpretation

After completing the field work, the data were processed and tabulated according to the requirements of the various aspects of the study.

The whole process of collection, serialisation and compilation of data was designed as carefully as possible. An amount of flexibility was retained in the design so that, in case of necessity, steps could be taken to modify the presentation of the material. The plan of presentation that finally emerged and the way of information has been embodied in the thesis is outlined below :

Plan of presentation

The findings of the study have been arranged under three parts. The first part, divided into three chapters, is concerned with the general background of the study. Chapter I sets forth the problems and methodology on the background of studies on women undertaken elsewhere in India. Chapter II provides an outline of the Assamese society with particular reference to women. The chapter also deals with the plural sociocultural context of Assam and its caste-based Hindu society in the Brahmaputra valley. Chapter III deals with the research setting, namely, Guwahati.

Part Two, comprising four chapters, is devoted to the profiles of the three categories of single women, namely, the widows, the divorced or separated women and the unmarried women. Chapter IV examines the social background of the respondents covered by the study. Chapters V, VI and VII delineate the ways in which the women acquire single status. Since the data relate to purely personal life and experience of the women, their names have been altered in the case studies to preserve their anonymity.

Part Three reviews the social horizon of the single women under five chapters. Chapter VIII examines the patterns of accommodation and living arrangement of the single women. Chapter IX is devoted to the analysis of the work situation of the single women. Chapter X provides an analysis of social and cultural contexts of the single women in contemporary Assamese Hindu society. An attempt has been made here to study the changing life of the single women from tradition to modernity. The chapter discusses the patterns of family, household and kinship of the single women and their life in relation to religion, recreation and other aspects. Chapter IX examines the position of single women in Assamese society under the provision of enacted legislations, relating specially to marriage, maintenance and succession. Chapter XII summarises the main findings by way of concluding observations and offers some suggestions regarding future course of action.

2

ASSAMESE SOCIETY AND WOMEN : AN OUTLINE

Assamese society in the context of North-East India

Assam is one of the norther-eastern States of India having certain regional peculiarities and distinctiveness. On the population front the State is characterised by a fusion of races and synthesis as well as co-existence of many cultures. "While being an integral part of India and sharing in the general life and culture of the country, Assam has, like all other component elements within the Unity that is India, its own special characteristics — its own particular *cachet*, so to say" (Chatterji 1959 :1).

On the physical front, the State comprises the territories of the Brahmaputra valley, the Barak valley and the two hill districts of Karbi Anglong and the North Cachar Hills. The total geographical area of the State is 78,582 km^2 (lying between latitudes 24° to 28^{0}N and longitudes 89°42′ to 96°30′ E) with a total population of 19,896,843 (projected figure, 1981 census).

Consequent upon the reorganisation of Assam in 1971, the State is bounded by other north-eastern States with predominant tribal populations and also by foreign countries like Bhutan and Bangladesh. The mighty Himalayas bound Assam in the north. On the northern and north-eastern borders of the State, there are the hills of Bhutan and Arunachal Pradesh, inhabited by a host of tribes having distinct cultures of their own. From the north-eastern and moving southward the State is bounded first by Nagaland, the land of various Naga tribes. To the extreme south, bordering Barak plains, is the State of Mizoram inhabited by the Mizo constellation of tribes. In the extreme south, the Barak plains of Assam is bounded by the State of Tripura. The Khasi, the Jaintia and the Garo hills, forming the State of Meghalaya, lie south of the Brahmaputra plains. On the western border there are the lowlying plains of Bangladesh. In the west, there is also a narrow corridor connecting the State with the northern part of the State of West Bengal (Fig. 2). Thus, surrounded on three sides by a chain of hills lies the valley of the mighty Brahmaputra, a long stretch, sprawling on both sides of the turbulent river. This valley constitutes the home of the Assamese speaking people and some other ethnic-cultural groups.

The Assam plains are divided into the Brahmaputra valley and the Barak valley. The Brahmaputra valley is divided (from east to west) into 18 administrative districts (Dhemaji, Lakhimpur, Tinsukia, Dibrugarh, Sibsagar, Jorhat, Golaghat, Sonitpur, Darrang, Nagaon, Marigaon, Kamrup, Nalbari, Barpeta, Bongaigaon, Kokrajhar, Goalpara and Dhubri).

The Barak valley is divided into the districts of Cachar, Hailakandi and Karimganj. In addition, there are the two hill districts, namely, Karbi-Anglong and North-Cachar Hills (Fig. 3). On the basis of geographical and cultural factors, Brahmaputra valley is again divisible into three regions : Upper Assam, Middle and Assam and Lower Assam. Upper Assam covers the districts in the extreme north-east and east, namely, Dhemaji, Lakhimpur, Tinsukia, Dibrugarh, Sibsagar, Jorhat and Golaghat. The districts of Sonitpur, Darrang, Nagaon and Marigaon may be placed in Middle Assam since these lie in the central stretch of the valley. Lower Assam is made up of Kamrup, Nalbari, Barpeta, Bongaigaon, Kokrajhar, Goalpara and Dhubri in the extreme west. 'Upper', 'Middle' and 'Lower' are terms used to connote the course of the mighty Brahmaputra flowing from the extreme north-east to the west. These terms also imply distinctive cultural regions in the context of Assam.

No satisfactory explanation has yet been found on the derivation of the name 'Assam'. "The term Assam, Asam or Aham was originally applied to the country ruled by the Ahoms, a Shan people who migrated from upper Burma at the beginning of the thirteenth century and gradually extended their rule throughout the Brahmaputra valley" (Cantlie 1984 : IX). Gait (1984 : 245-6) opines that the term 'Asama' which means 'unequalled' or 'peerless' was applied to the Shans by the local people as they conquered the country with their superior might. From the word 'Asama' the word Assam might with greater probability have been derived. The conquering tribe's new appellation 'Asama' itself later on degenerated to the word 'Ahom'. Kakati (1987 : 3) suggests that '...Asama, peerless, may be a latter day Sanskritisation of some earlier form like Acham.' According to him, in Tai language 'cham' means 'to be defeated'. With the addition of an Assamese prefix 'A', it became 'Acham' to mean 'undefeated', 'conquerors'.

Socio-historical background of Assamese society

i. *Ethnic composition* :

It is difficult to say, who were the original inhabitants of Assam. Ethnically the Assamese people are of mixed origin. Various racial elements have entered into its composition. According to Das (1987 : 3) the people of Assasm are usually the people whose mother tongue is Assamese and the indigenous tribal inhabitants of this part of the country. He divides the people of Assam into two broad categories : tribal and non-tribal.

According to the Census of 1971, Assam's tribal population was a little over 1.6 million, comprising 10.99 per cent of the total population. The majority, 1.34 million in 1971, of the tribals belong to the nine recognised scheduled tribes of the plains. These are the Bodo-kachari, Miri (or Mishing), Sonowal and other Kachari, Rabha, Lalung, Deori, Barmans of Cachar, Mech and the Hojai. The scheduled tribes of the hills are the Mikir (or Karbi), the Dimasa and small groups of Naga, Kuki, Mizo, Jaintia and a few other tribal affiliations (Bhagabati 1988 : 20).

The non-tribal population of Assam includes : (i) Certain Mongoloid populations like the Ahom, Chutiya, Moran and the Koch, which are not included under scheduled tribes but considered as 'Other Backward Classes', (ii) the 'Caste Hindu', (iii) the scheduled castes, (iv) the Muslims and a small number of Assamese Sikhs, Christians and Jains.

Besides the above mentioned populations, there are Bengali

speaking communities and other Indians who have come and settled in Assam at different times. To quote Cantlie (1984 : ix-x) :

"The term 'Assamese' is sometimes used to refer to those who are citizens of Assam:in this sense it includes tea-garden labour and Mymensinghi settlers. More generally, however, it is used to denote the indigenous or long-settled inhabitants who are recognized as Assamese, not only in language, but also in culture and way of life."

Das also points (1987:5) to the large number of tea-garden labourers and people from erstwhile East Bengal, more particularly from Mymeshing district who form a section of the people of Assam. In language, in their way of life, some of the tea-garden labourers have become indistinguishable from the local Assamese people. Thus it is evident that there has been a series of migration into Assam in the pre-modern and modern times to give rise to the wider Assamese population. Das further points out that in the population of Assam two major races, Mongoloids and Caucasoids, are living side by side since long past. To quote him, "... a glance at the racial elements in the population of Assam reveals that Assam is a meeting place of various ethnic stocks having diverse socio-cultural backgrounds who came to this part of the country in different times from different directions" (Das 1987:63).

Through a process of active assimilation of diverse races and cultures represented by numerous small ethnic groups, Assam has come to acquire its unique socio-cultural identity. There has been a gradual evolution of a homogeneous entity out of the mixing of diverse cultures. This homogeneous entity has developed into a distinct community called Assamese or *Assamiya* with its distinctive culture and tradition.

ii. *Language* :

Assamese is the mother tongue of the Assamese people. Out of the total population of Assam, 60.88 per cent of people speak Assamese language (Census 1971). Choudhury (1987:365) has traced the origin of this language in the epigraphs of the seventh century A.D. and later. Barua (1959:56) also opines that it is developed out of Sanskrit language as early as the seventh century A.D. Scholars like Grierson and S.K. Chatterjee were of the opinion that the languages originated from the Magadhan Prakrit.

Explaining the affinities of Assamese language, Kakati (1987: 11) opines that Assamese is "... an independent speech related to Bengali, both occupying the position of dialects with reference to some standard Magadhan *Apabhramsa.*" He also mentions how the Austric, Kolerian, Malayalam, Bodo and other elements have enriched Assamese vocabulary.

The numerous non-Aryan dialects of Assam belong mainly to the Tibeto-Burman linguistic family. Many of these groups (e.g. the Chutiya and Ahom) have abandoned their original speeches or dialects in the course of time and have adopted the Indo-Aryan Assamese language as their mother tongue.

Some tribal groups of Assam, such as the Bodo-Kachari, the Mishing (Miri) and the Karbi (Mikir) who are inhabitants of the Brahmaputra valley and neighbouring hill regions of Assam have retained their respective languages. Though the process of 'Assamisation' of indigenous tribals has been an age-old phenomenon in Assam, it has considerably weakened in the recent years. Explaining the significant role played by the plains tribals of Assam in the formation of the regional Assamese society, Bhagabati (1988:21) points out :

"One now notices a rejection by many of these tribes of the composite 'Assamese identity' the core element of which was the adoption of Assamese language .... On the cultural front, language has emerged as one of the major issues among those tribes who were so long subsumed under the wider Assamese nationality." They, however, use Assamese for communication with other sections of the regional population.

iii. *Religion*

The religious life of the people of Assam has been dominated by Hinduism from the ancient times. According to the 1971 census, 71.04 per cent of the people of Assam are Hindus.

The Hindu priests and the warriors found their way to Assam and settled in the Brahmaputra valley under royal patronage at different periods of history. The old tribal beliefs of the inhabitants were gradually eroded and the Hindu priests established their influence over the religious practices of the indigenous inhabitants. Blood sacrifice and idol worship were already in vogue, and now Siva, Durga and Kali came to be the dominant deities. But the development of the Vaishnavite faith in the fifteenth century

(Sarma 1959:50) was a turning point in the religious history of Assam. Sankardeva, the leader of the Vaishnava renaissance in Assam and the founder of the *satra* institution preached a pure and simple form of Hinduism. It is the religion of the worship of one God (Vishnu) through recitation of His name, in hymns and prayers. "The official name of the bhakti creed of Sankardeva is ekasarana namadharma, and this explains its cardinal principles, which enjoin the worship of one god, that is, Vishnu, especially in the incarnation of Krsna, and interdicts the votaries from the worship of any other deity ..." (Neog 1959:37).

The *satras* till today have remained as centres of religious education and religious activities of the Vaishavite communities of the Assamese Hindus.

In Assam, the centre of all Vaishnavite religious activities is the *namghar* (prayer house). It is an integral part of the social machinery by which villagers are enabled to live together in an orderly arrangement of social relations. Besides performing the religious ceremonies in the *namghar*, the villagers use it as a public place to discuss the affairs of the village.

Women are generally not debarred from participation in any socio-religious activities. Elderly women go to *namghar* to recite *nam-kirttan* (devotional song). In the Assamese Hindu villages every household has a *thapana* (altar) or a *gosai-ghar* (prayer room) where women offer daily prayer.

According to the census of 1971, the Muslims constitute 24.03 per cent of the total population of the State. The Muslim saint popularly known as Azan Fakir came to Assam in the middle of the seventeenth century who stabilized Islam in Assam. Many local people were converted to Islam because of the influence of this Muslim saint (Das 1987:7).

The Assamese Hindus and Muslims share many common socio-cultural characteristics. "Besides observing the Muslim religious observances they have been observing many Assamese social festivals from early times" (Sarma 1981:120). The reason, as pointed out by Das, is that, many conversions generally took place through marriage and there was no large-scale migration of Muslims to Assam in the past. They came in small numbers in different periods and gradually became part of the greater Assamese community (Das 1987:7).

Christianity came to Assam after the British annexation in 1826. However, Christians constitute only 4.46 per cent of the total population of the State (1971 Census) and most of them belong to tribal communities.

There is a small community of Sikhs whose mother tongue is Assamese. The Assamese Sikhs are mainly concentrated in Nagaon.

In addition to the above, there are a few small Buddhist populations in Uppper Assam, e.g., the Khamyang Aiton, Tai Phake, Turung and the Duania.

iv. *Economy* :

Assamese society is basically a peasant society. Agriculture is the mainstay of the Assamese people. Eighty per cent of the State's population is dependent on agriculture. Out of the total working population, 66 per cent are engaged in agriculture (Statistical Handbook of Assam, 1984 : 32). Apart from agriculture, the following subsidiary occupations are also important in Assam.

Weaving in handlooms is widely undertaken by the rural women of Assam. As a household level industry it employs a large number of indigenous Assamese women. According to a survey conducted during 1975-76, there were 6.94 lakh handlooms and 7.86 lakh persons engaged in weaving (*Assam Information,* 1983). Handloom is inextricably linked with the culture and traditions of Assam.

Another vocation in rural Assam is rearing of silk worm and production of *endi, muga* and *pat* silk yarn. Sericulture has been practised from the time immemorial, especially by the womenfolk of Assam. The yarn is also used for weaving of the three varieties of silk fabrics. However, now-a-days weaving of silk at household level is on the wane. Silk is mostly produced commercially in certain recognised production centres.

Cane and bamboo crafts and brass and bell metal industry also occupy places of pride in the economic life of the people.

Assam is famous for production of tea. Almost half of the tea produced in India is grown in Assam. There are 770 tea gardens in Assam (Statistical Handbook of Assam 1982).

Assam is rich in natural resources. It supplies 60 per cent of the country's crude oil from her oil fields and a considerable percentage of coal from her coal fields. Timber and plywood are notable contributions of the State to the economy of India.

Social network

i. *The Caste system* :

Caste is an important aspect of Assamese Hindu society. However, the caste system in Assam is not as elaborately developed as it is in many other parts of India. The castes are hierarchically arranged but the internal lives of differences are not so very rigid. There are various reasons for the liberal ethos of the Assamese Hindu society. One reason might be the influence of the preachings of Sankardeva, the religious reformist of the fifteenth century in the Brahmaputra valley of Assam. "In his religious order caste was dethroned and this liberal philosophy of neo-Vaishnavite faith attracted people irrespective of caste, creed, religion and tribe. The principles of equality and fraternity thus formed an embedded part of the socio-cultural life of the people of the Valley" (Dev and Lahiri 1984 : XV). Another reason for the absence of a rigid caste system is that "... Assam came under the influence of the Aryan culture at a much later date and hence casteism could not gain strong foothold" (Das 1987 : 11).

In general practice, the Assamese Hindus can broadly be divided into two categories. To quote Das (1987:12), "These are the 'Bamun' (Brahmin) and the 'Sudir' (Sudra ; non-Brahmin). The Sudir group includes several castes of different hierarchical positions."

The *Brahmins* and the other upper castes of the Hindus enjoyed in the past a privileged position in society. Traditionally, the Brahmins maintain their social exclusiveness as a caste more rigidly than any other caste groups of Assam. They do not plough by themselves, nor would interdine and marry in other castes. There are certain prohibitions required to be observed by the Brahmin widows. Tradition prohibits them from marrying and eating of fish and meat. Priestly service and pursuit of learning are the traditional calling of the Brahmins.

The Kayasthas occupy a distinctive position in traditional Assamese society. They are believed to be Kshatriya and there are old references to them as officers and scribes (Barooah 1978 : 113). They also do not plough by themselves.

The Kalita is another prominent caste of Assam. They were once a powerful caste who equated themselves with Kshatriyas in ancient Assam (*ibid.*:114).

The Koch, an agricultural caste of Assam, has been described in the Gazetteer of India as "an aboriginal tribe, apparently of Mongolian origin" (*ibid.*).

The Ahoms occupy a distinct position in the Hindu social order of the Assamese society. The ancestors of the present day Ahoms migrated in Assam in the early part of the thirteenth century and settled in the Brahmaputra valley as a ruling elite class. Gradually the beliefs and rituals of the traditional Ahoms were replaced by the Hindu customs and ceremonies and ultimately they adopted Hinduism. Though the Ahoms are well-established Hindus, they maintain a distinct identity of their own within the present day Hindu society.

The total number of scheduled castes in Assam as a whole comes to sixteen, constituting only 6.2 per cent of the State's total population (Census, 1971). The Kaibarttas, whose traditional calling is fishing, is a distinct caste belonging to the scheduled caste category. According to the census of 1971, the percentage of this caste is 35.3 out of the total scheduled caste population of Assam. Most of the members of this community are followers of Vaishnavism.

Namasudra, Patni, Malo, Hira, Bania, Dhubi are some other scheduled caste communities of Assam.

In addition to the castes mentioned above, there are many other castes like Baria, Sut, Yogi, Vaishya, Saloi and Keot in different parts of Assam.

In the changing Assamese society, difference in caste or subcaste is not considered an insurmountable barrier to social amity and intercourse. Datta (1980 : 62) has analyzed the liberalism of the Assamese folkmind in the caste-based society. According to him, except in the case of Brahmins and one or two other 'higher-castes', caste position has not been well-defined in Assam and inter-caste communication at all levels has been fairly easy.

One of the notable features of the caste system of Assam is the relative weakness of the notions and practices relating to untouchability. "Untouchability has never been a big problem in the

Assamese society and the social stigma attached to some of the so-called lowly professions has been practically absent" (Datta 1981: 10). In this, there is a sharp contrast to the situation in some other parts of India. The relative absence of untouchability in the Assamese society was chiefly due to two factors : (a) The looseness of caste organisation, in an essentially tribal social matrix and (b) the teachings of the great Vaishnava Guru Sankardeva and his associates. The effective functioning of a large number of Vaishnava *satras* throughout the Brahmaputra valley helped to minimise notions of untouchability. Thus to quote one scholar, "In the Vaisnava congregation all members of the fraternity were equal. The prayer services and the reading of sacred texts could be conducted by person able to do it, irrespective of his social standing in the old scale. The offerings to the deity could be distributed in the assembly by men of any caste within the circle of bhaktas. Notwithstanding persecution from the old orthodoxy, people flocked to Sankardeva's side to listen to the message of Love, and met there as equal sons of God" (Neog : 1959 : 39).

The Bihu, which is the most important folk festival of Assam cutting across caste lines, indicates the liberal attitude of the Assamese people. This traditional festival is celebrated by people of all castes and also by various tribal communities of the Assam plains in one form or another. During the festival, every Assamese family receives and entertains the visitors irrespective of caste, creed or community.

ii. *Family and Marriage* :

Due to urbanisation, spread of formal education and increasing diversification of occupation, the age-old sentiment of joint family in Assam has undergone significant changes. There is a clear trend towards emergence of nuclear family. This is more noticeable in the urban areas than in the villages.

The Assamese Hindu society is patrilineal. Hence in the context of the family, there is a clear emphasis on the male line in regard to descent, inheritance, residence rules. The children thus belong to the *gotra* of their father though girls after marriage become affiliated to their respective husbands' *gotra.* The pattern of authority within the family is clearly patripotestal so that a man is in control over domestic matters. He also has great responsibilities towards his wife, children and other members of the family. For example, in the maintenance, education and marriage of the children, the man has to shoulder comparatively greater responsibilities than his wife. If for some reasons a daughter remains unmarried or if a daughter becomes a widow who cannot obtain any support from her husband's family, she has to be looked after by her father. After his death, generally the eldest son of the family occupies his place as the head. A sense of economic obligation is always there among the members of a family. Even if a joint family is physically dispersed, a son or a brother, working away from home, is generally expected to contribute according to his means to the family coffers.

In term of living arrangement, the definition of a household in Assam can be given by the nature of arrangment for food. In a recent study, Cantlie has also pointed out that "... commanality is seen as the defining criterion of a single family. In every household there is one kitchen and one rice pounder. Division is understood as eating separately" (Cantlie 1984:37).

Children are married in order of seniority in the family. Among the high caste Assamese Hindus, Brahma form of marriage is the common practice. This type of marriage is arranged by way of negotiation between the families of the bride and the groom. The father or any other guardian of the bride performs the *sampradan* (giving away) ceremony in front of the sacred fire (i.e., *homa*) as per Vedic rites.

Marriage within the same caste, i.e., endogamy is the general rule of the Assamese Hindu society. But marriage within the same *gotra* is prohibited. Marriage between certain categories of kin is prohibited. For any person the degree of prohibition is up to seven generations on the father's side and on the mother's side it is up to five generations.

Hypergamous (*anuloma*) marriage, where a man from a higher caste can marry a girl from a lower caste is approved by society; but hypogamous *(pratiloma)* marriage does not receive a similar approval. Inter-caste marriages are, however, becoming common. Pointing out a *Bihu* folk song, Datta (1980 : 62) asserts that even in the field of matrimony, caste bars have normally not been unsurmountable :

> "If you so desire and I so desire,
> what can the Kalita caste do?"
> (toro mane gole, more mane gole,
> ki kariba Kalita kule?)

Thus goes a popular *Bihu* folk song. The implication is obvious."

The practice of dowry is not prevalent in the traditional Assamese society. This indicates a fair degree of freedom that a woman enjoys in society. But it is an established custom to give certain essential articles as gifts to the bride by her family. Such gifts include clothes, ornaments, utensils, furniture and other necessary articles to set up a home. A few sets of clothes and if possible, gold ornaments are also given to the bride from the bride groom's family at a pre-wedding ceremony.

In case of tribal villages the sytem of bride price which is the reverse of dowry system, is in vogue. Payment of bride price in the form of cash is nominal; but payment in kind, such as cattles, implements, articles of clothing and utensils to the bride's family is rather heavy.

Monogamy is the general rule among the Assamese society. The practice of polygamy, though found in some of the villages, is not very common nowadays.

Marriage is regarded as indissoluble tie between the husband and wife in the traditional Assamese society. But dissolution of marriage by way of separation or divorce is nowadays becoming evident. In rural areas of Assam, this class of women has a low status in society. It is not possible for them to think of remarriage where traditions and customs to the contrary prevail. But in urban society such women often marry again without bothering about any social disapproval.

Widows in traditional Assamese society have been subjected to certain restrictions and taboos. There are certain prohibitions strictly followed more by the widows of the Brahmin caste than by those of the other castes. A Brahmin widow's remarriage is hardly possible in the rural society due to social disapproval. Remarriage of widows to some other castes is not so strongly frowned upon. Sometimes it is seen that a widowed or divorced woman can enter into a form of common-law union with a man and they stay together as husband and wife without performing any formal marriage rituals.

Place of women in Assamese society

In seeking to understand the social role of women and the

place they have traditionally occupied in the Assamese society, it is necessary to briefly consider references in history to women. History provides us with some idea of the lives of Assamese women in general as well as of those who made their mark in different spheres of social life.

i. *Historical background* :

The social and the prestige bestowed on women in the Ahom period (1228-1826) appear to have been fairly high. The Ahom princesses took prominent part not only on ceremonial occasions, but they also exercised considerable influence in the affairs of the State. There are references to the heroic deeds of Assamese women of courage and determination in different periods.

For instance, Mula Gabharu, the consort of the Ahom Commander-in-Chief Phra-Shen-Mong Bar-Gohain, rushed to the battlefield with sword in her hand when the Muslim invaders attempted to conquer the Ahom Kingdom in the year 1532 (Gogoi 1968 : 299). She tried to avenge the death of her husband and died fighting in the battlefield (Bhuyan 1965 : 71).

Another woman of repute in Assam history was Ramani Gabhoru, daughter of King Jayadhwaj Singha who had been given in marriage to the royal family of Emperor Aurangzeb in 1663 A.D. Her maternal uncle, Laluk Barphukan, had conspired to surrender Guwahati to the Moghuls. Ramani, therefore, living in the Moghul viceregal palace near Dhaka, wrote to her uncle to desist from such as unpartriotic act (*ibid.*:71).

The image of Jaymati Kunwari comes next before us. She was the faithful wife of the Ahom prince Gadapani of Tungkhungia royal family and mother of Rudra Singha, the great Ahom king. Gadapani had good claims to the throne and he was also a prince of extra-ordinary physical vigour, ability and courage. When king Lara Raja (who ruled from 1679 to 1681) determined to kill all the descendants of former king whom he feared as probable contenders to the throne, spies were employed to track Gadapani and capture him. Gadapani had meanwhile left home fearing capture. Under the orders of Lara Raja, Jaymati was captured and tortured to death for refusing to divulge the whereabouts of her fugitive husband (Gogoi 1968 : 495). Gadapani, later on became the king (1681-1696) as Gadadhar Singha.

It would thus be proper to infer that women, particularly at higher levels of society, could yield considerable power and also initiate action on their own. There is a clear continuity of the tradition as exemplified by the cases of Phuleswari and Ambika.

Phuleswari was the principal queen as declared by her hus band, king Siva Singha (1714-1744). As stated by Gait (1984 : 184), "Phuleswari's authority was far from normal. She was even more under the influence of the Brahmans than her husband." She even suppressed the age-old Ahom custom of burying the dead and compelled them to follow the Hindu custom of cremation. "There was no freedom of conscience under her regime" (Gogoi 1968 : 511). Phuleswari was responsible for having a magnificent tank called Gaurisagar excavated in Sibsagar district with three different temples built on its bank. She died in 1731 A.D. The king then married her sister Draupadi giving her name Ambika. Following her sister's example, Ambika Devi arranged excavation of the second biggest and most famous tank in Assam, called Sivasagar in 1733 A.D. with three big temples side by side on its bank in the same year. One of them is an impressive Siva temple, with large gold-covered dome. It is the biggest and tallest of the temples in Assam (*ibid.* : 512). The inscriptions of the coins issued between 1724 and 1731, and 1732 and 1736 A.D. bear the name of Phuleswari and Ambika, respectively along with the name of Siva Singha (*ibid.*: 513). This can be taken as an indication of the acceptance of women's high status among the nobility of Assam.

These instances from history still inspire the people of Assam. The indomitable courage and unwavering adherence to values and ideals of society shown by women in historical times is very much a part and parcel of Assamese lore.

But the Burmese invasion of Assam (1817 A.D.) caused a set back in the position of women in Assam. Describing the deplorable condition of the people under the Burmese, Gait (1984: 231) opined : "The oppressions of the Burmese became more and more unbearable, and no one could be sure of his wealth or reputation, or even of his life. Not only did they rob everyone who had anything worth taking, but they wantonly burnt down villages, and even temples, violated the chastity of women, old and young alike, and put large numbers of innocent persons to death."

The atrocities perpetrated by the Burmese invaders on the local populace during those years of turmoil (Burmese ravages took place from 1819 to 1824 A.D.) seem to have pushed the women from the public arena into the domestic arena where they became somewhat less prominent and invisible.

Following the British annexation in 1826 A.D., Assam came into closer and more effective contact with the rest of India. Assam's cultural and political life including the lives of women, came to be strongly influenced by changes introduced from outside the region.

Many accounts of the early British period (1826-1870 A.D.) describe the position of women prevailing at that time. Orunodoi, a monthly paper in Assamese, edited by the American Baptist Missionary Rev. Nathan Brown, which first appeared in 1846, was an important forum for such accounts. There were articles reflecting on the position of women in Assamese society in the 19th century (Neog 1983, compiled : *Orunodoi* 1846-54).

Sati, the practice of self-immolation by the widow in the bruning pyre of the deceased husband, was a rare phenomenon in Assam. A case on record was of a wife from a village in the southern part of Sibsagar district. She was preparing herself for *sati,* but the timely intervention of police prevented her from the act on 26 April, 1846 (*ibid.* : 36).

The British introduced the new system of English education with establishment of Guwahati Seminary in 1835 (Sarma 1981 : 113). Since then several English schools came to be established in different places of Assam. The gradual percolation of English education introduced new ideas and values in the Assamese society. The new generation of educated youths of the early nineteeth century pointed out many evil practices and superstitions prevalent in society. They were also influenced by the progressive ideas of writers and social reformers of their time in neighbouring Bengal like Raja Rammohan Roy (1772-1833), Isvarachandra Vidyasagar (1820-1891) and Bankim Chandra Chatterjee (1838-1894). The problem of widow remarriage and the practice of early marriage attracted the attention of the educated youth of 19th and early 20th century Assam. The small but vocal educated class made up of men like Anandaram Dhekial Phukan, Gunabhiram Barua, Hemchandra Barua, Lakhminath Bejbaruah, pleaded for widow remarriage and abolition of child marriage in the Assamese society in their many and varied writings (*ibid.*: 114).

Raibahadur Gunabhiram Barua (1834-1894) was an eye-witness to the first widow remarriage celebrated in the presence of Isvarachandra Vidyasagar in Calcutta in 1856 (Misra 1987:113). He was so moved by that event that he wrote a play named, *Ram-Navami* in 1857, supporting the remarriage of young Brahmin widows. He himself set an example by marrying a widow in 1870. It was the first case of widow remarriage by an Assamese Brahmin (Saikia, compiled, 1984 *Assam Bandhu* : 20). He was also the first Assamese to send his nine-year-old daughter to Calcutta for higher education (Misra 1987 : 112). Gunabhiram advocated for women's emancipation through *Orunodoi* and *Assam Bandhu* (1885-1886) the magazine edited by himself. He was a close relative of Anandaram Dhekial Phukan (*ibid.* : 111). Anandaram "... was also in favour of remarriage of widow by setting himself marrying a widow" (Acharyya 1987:251).

Another nineteenth century social rebel was Hemchandra Barua. He himself was a strong advocate of widow-remarriage and "... refused to marry a second time after the death of his wife in protest against the prevalent social injustice to women in the Hindu society" (Misra 1987 : 118).

Lakshminath Bezbarua, a stalwart of Assamese literature, expressed his awareness of the position of women in Assamese Hindu society in many of his short stories. He also wrote in favour of widow-remarriage.

In Assam, particularly in the upper castes, the notion of early marriage for girls appear to have been deeply entrenched. It seems that the people thought that girls were born into a family only to be given away in marriage as early as possible. Thus, to quote a nineteenth century writer: "In Assam it is reckoned a disgrace to a family to have a daughter unmarried after the age of puberty; but in the lower castes many young women do not succeed in getting husbands till the age of twenty" (M'Cosh 1975 : 22).

Among the Brahmin and Kayastha families, girls were married off between ten and fouteen years of age, i.e., before the attainment of puberty (Sarma 1981:118). Child marriage was perhaps rare among other castes. Even to this day, Brahmin girls in the rural areas are married off at an early age unlike among other castes.

ii. *Growth and development of female education* :

Formal education was not considered relevant for girls. It

appears from certain accounts that in the early years of British rule, the Assamese people did not think of the necessity of education for women (Robinson 1975 : 277). "The Christian Missionaries like Mrs. Brown, Cutter, Robinson and Barker had initiated for setting up schools for girls. The first girls' school was opened at Sibsagar in 1840 and then at Nowgong and Guwahati consequently. However, many young girls of orthodox background had lost their privilege of attending schools and their social barrier had stood as obstacles to their freedom and progress" (Acharyya 1987 : 258). But there are indications that till the 1850s, there was little or no female education in Assam (Neog compiled 1983 : *Orunodoi* : 1042). Due to the practice of child marriage, most girls were withdrawn from school at an early age. Some attention to female education began to be paid from the late nineteenth century under the leadership of a few enlightened persons of Assam. They pleaded for female education in popular magazines like *Assam Bandhu* (first appeared in 1885), *Mou* (first appeared in 1886) and newspapers like *Assamese News* (first appeared in 1880). Anandaram Dhekial Phukan was one of them who advocated the emancipation of women through education (Acharyya 1987 : 251)

Though there were no schools for girls in the early years of the growth of education in Assam, instruction was given to them perhaps at home by parents or guardians or by paid instructors. A few women who could read and write thus emerged even without formal schooling. "For instance, Padmavati Devi Phukanani wrote a novel *Sudharmar Upakhyan* which was published in 1884" (Lahkar 1987 : 2).

In 1870 there were eight girls' schools in Assam, five in Kamrup and one each in Darrang, Nowgong and Lakhimpur districts (*ibid.* : 3). Even at the turn of the nineteenth century, scope for female education in Assam was practically non-existing. In the absence of any higher educational institutions for women in Assam, Debiprava Bhuyan, a progressive woman had to take her two daughters, Durgaprava and Hemaprava, to Calcutta to study in Bethune School. Hemaprava studied there up to B.A. level and got married in the year 1906. Later on, she bacame the head mistress of Dibrugarh Girls' Model School in the year 1913. It is through her effort that this school was upgraded to a high school. Incidentally, this was the first girls' high school in Assam. Her daughter Amalprava Das was the first Assamese woman to obtain a Master's degree in science (Chemistry) in 1935 (Miri ed : 1975).

Another educated woman was Kadambini Saikia who passed her middle school examination from Nowgong in 1916. She was the only girl student of her school at that time (*ibid.*). By the year 1929-30 girls were found to be appearing in the B.A. examination also (Lahkar : 1987 : 120). Another illustrious woman of the early part of this century was Rajabala Das. She tried for spreading female education in Assam. She was the founder of Panbazar Girls' High School and Handique Girls' College, both located at Guwahati. She started the college in 1939 only with two girl students (Miri ed : 1975).

In 1901, the percentage of women literacy stood at only 0.59. In 1931, it was below 2 per cent. In 1941, it was 4.38 per cent (Lahkar 1987 : 42). There was a steady, though rather slow, growth of female education in Assam in the first half of the present century so that by 1951, the percentage of literate women in Assam rose to 9.48 per cent. It was only after Independence that women's education made notable progress. By 1961 and 1971, this percentage rose to 19.21 and 23.52, respectively.

iii. *Household and economic activities of women* :

In the traditional Assamese society, women were primarily engaged in household duties and other economic activities. There was no scope for formal education of women in the structure of the Assamese society. They had to be engaged, without much leisure, in various domestic activities : cleaning and sweeping, washing, cooking and distributing meals, rearing children and looking after the comforts of the members of their households. In addition, women of cultivating castes and communities worked in the field, particularly in transplantation, weeding and harvesting of paddy. Husking of paddy, with the help of *dhenki* (wooden husking lever plied by feet) or *ural* (wooden mortar and pestle), was a regular feminine task. But with the introduction of rice mills in the last few decades in most part of rural Assam, many women have been freed from this traditional work.

In tribal villages, agricultural activities of womenfolk are still heavier. They participate in hoeing, planting, weeding, tending crops, harvesting and carrying the harvest home on their heads. They also have to look after the livestock and poultry. As the tribal people do not usually rear cattle for milk, milking is not a part of their traditional work. In non-tribal peasant villages, however, milking is usually done by the women.

The fetching of water and collection of firewood are exclusively done by women in the tribal villages. Fishing for family consumption is another activity performed by the womenfolk of some tribal communities of Assam.

Besides other domestic chores, weaving has been a specific feminine occupation throughout Assam since early times. As an Assamese historian of repute notes : "A unique feature of Assamese society is the absence of any specific class reserved only for weaving. Every Assamese woman, be she the daughter of a Brahman or a Sudra, a Buddhist or an animist, a Muhammedan or a Christian, a prince or a beggar, is a weaver by birth. A knowledge of weaving is an essential qualification for her, while proficiency in the art ensures for her a ready disposal in the matrimonial market" (Bhuyan 1965:66). In the historical times, it was a popular belief that the wearing apparel spun and woven in the course of a single night by the wife served her warrior husband as a *kabacha* (i.e., life saving garment). It was believed that *kabacha* cloth would earn him victory in war (Bar Barua 1981:54).

Before the advent of British rule, cloth for home consumption was not imported from out side, but produced in every household, irrespective of caste and community. Every Assamese family, specially in the rural areas, was expected to keep a handloom, and the women were expected to be expert weavers. Knowledge of weaving has traditionally been regarded as a matter of prestige for an Assamese woman.

Since Independence, certain changes have taken place in the traditional Assamese Hindu society and along with these the role and status of Assamese women, too, have changed. In the recent years, embroidery, knitting, cutting and sewing have become popular among the Assamese women even in the rural areas.

In addition to traditional household work, a small number of Assamese women are nowadays engaged in gainful activities including wage-earning and salaried jobs outside their homes. Though for women working outside the domestic and agricultural spheres were once considered as derogatory to the prestige of the family, the idea has now disappeared to a great extent due to spread of education, and also the felt need for additional cash income. There is a distinct trend now among educated Assamese women to seek job to fulfil status and economic aspirations. There appears to be a clear preference for teaching jobs among the educated Assamese women. However, many of them are to be found in non teaching jobs in various Government and non-Government sectors. Since 1969, some women have also been working in police and home-guards department of Assam.

iv. *Women in the context of kinship* :

In Assamese kinship system, the two categories of kin, affines and agnates, are collectively referred to as *mitir-kutumb.* As the anthropologist Cantlie (1984:25) notes, "*The kutumb* is usually identified with the agnatic line or house (*bamsa*) and *bamsa* connected by marriage become affines (*mitir*) of one another."

The women occupy an important position in the traditional Assamese kinship system. The culturally defined patterns of kinship behaviour towards womenfolk having distinctive roles as mother, sister, wife, daughter, etc., are marked by respect, obedience, affection, obligation, love and cordiality. However, there are certain restrictions imposed on women at certain stages of their life and there are also clear indications in the kinship system of their subservient position to menfolk. After the attainment of her puberty, a girl is considered to be impure till her marriage. In the traditional families, an elderly person usually does not take food cooked by a grownup unmarried girl (*ibid.* : 51). A widow also carries the burden of being considered inauspicious on certain ceremonial occasions, such as weddings, where she is debarred from many rites. In different kinship roles, e.g., as wife, daughter and sister, a woman has to be under the authority of menfolk and are generally expected to abide by men's decision in various matters. The married women are required to observe certain rules of avoidance, particularly in regard to menfolk of the husband's family. For instance, a woman cannot utter the name of her husband; she cannot talk directly to her husband's elder brothers and she has to behave in a subdued fashion, showing due respect while interacting with senior members of her husband's family. But she does not have to observe such avoidances and respectfulness towards the relations junior to her husband. In the non-tribal Assamese Hindu villages, a daughter-in-law always keeps her head covered with the upper piece of her *chadar* as a mark of showing due respect to elders. In the traditional kinship context, the mother-in-law exercises a great deal of control over the daughter-in-law. Sometimes, her relationship with the daughter-in-law is found to be strained. The relationships of a woman with her husband's younger brother and her elder sisters' husbands are marked by innocent joking and easy interaction.

A man usually consults his wife in taking decisions on important matters concerning the children and the family. She usually takes active part in the settlement of marriage of children, purchase and sale of land, construction or extension of dwelling house and education of the children.

Women in the rural areas generally cannot buy and sell on their own without consent or approval of their husbands. They usually do not get the opportunity for the purchase of household requirements nor is it considered 'proper' for women to go out to *hats* and bazaars. All household requirements, including women's and children's garments, are purchased by the male members of the family. But Assamese women in the semi-urban and urban areas have greater freedom and opportunity in this respect.

v. *Women in public sphere* :

Despite their somewhat subservient status in history, especially since the Burmese invasion in the early nineteenth century, the rural women of Assam have always been remarkably free in regard to movements and outdoor activities. In this, a clear contrast can be seen with rural women of other parts of India. This relative freedom is epitomised by the absence of the *purdah* system which is attributed by some to strong Islamic influence in other parts of India. From early records on Assam it is found that the practice of confinement of women within the family circle and under veil had never existed in Assam. Accounts of Muhammedan foreign traveller, Shihabuddin, who accomplished Mir Jumlah in his Assam expedition in 1662, confirms this view. Giving a comprehensive description of the people and the country, he observed (Gait 1984:146), "The wives of the Rajas and peasants alike never veil their faces before anybody, and they move about in the market places with bare heads." Robinson (1975:254) also recorded his impression in the same vein. The clear persistence of essentially tribal values and ideology among the Assamese peasantry explains the freedom enjoyed by the women. The caste system, though prevalent is not as rigid with regard to its taboos and restrictions as it is in other parts of India.

It will not be wrong to surmise that absence of rigid restrictions on women in the past have aided their participation in public life to a great extent. Influenced by the progressive ideas current in the early twentieth century, some educated Assamese women proposed to form a women's association (*mahila samiti*) in the State to promote women's welfare and interest. Through the efforts of women like Debiprava Bhuyan and her daughter, Hemaprava Das, a *mahila samiti* was formed in 1915 at Dibrugarh. Next, a similar *samiti* was formed at Nagaon in 1917 with Khagendrapriya Baruani and Swarnalata Barua as president and secretary, respectively (Barua 1975:22).

In the Assam *chatra sanmilan* (i.e., students conventions) held at Tezpur in 1918, Assamese girls participated as student members for the first time. In 1919, another *mahila samiti* was formed at Tezpur under the leadership of Chandraprava Saikiani, one of the active participants of *chhatra sanmilan (ibid.)*.

An all Assam formal association of women, the *Assam Mahila Samiti*, was formed in 1926 and Chandraprava Saikiani became its president (*ibid.* : 23).

These institutions, organised by women and for the benefit of women, tried to create public opinion against social evils like the practice of child marriage and polygamy. They took prompt action in such matters by way of issuing 'cancellation notices' on behalf of the *samiti*. For such actions, the *mahila samiti* was sometimes called *biya bhanga samiti* (marriage cancelling organization) in the early part of this century (*ibid.* : 24).

The women, through this institution, also protested against the *Purdah* system which had crept into the Assamese society to some extent in later years. For instance, in public places, the women were not allowed to sit along with men. In the 1925 session of *Asam Sahitya Sabha* (the premier socio-literary organization of Assam) held at Nagaon, Chandraprava Saikiani created history by pulling down the bamboo screen isolating women from men (*ibid.*).

Thus, by early 1930s a small section of educated Assamese women paved the way for increasing participation of women in public spheres. The socio-political ferment of movement for Indian Independence also created an atmosphere for feminine participation in arenas outside the traditional sphere of the household. Many Assamese women worked alongside men in the country's struggle for freedom. The non-co-operation movement included actions like boycotting of foreign goods, mainly foreign cloth and garments, emphasizing the promotion of *swadeshi*. "It was resolved that the demands for foreign cloth should be replaced by hand-spun and hand-woven khadi." (Bhuyan et. al. eds. 1978 : 218). As Assam was known for home-spinning and weaving, *the non-co-operators began to undertake an intensive constructive programme for khadi* in the villages. These were the women who by their zeal and sacrifice introduced the *charkha* in almost every household to produce *khadi*. Gandhiji, in his visit to Assam in 1921, was highly pleased to witness that weaving was a common household-level undertaking of Assamese womenfolk. He expressed his opinion in an article, 'Lovely Assam', published in *Young India*, in the following words :

"Every woman of Assam is a born weaver. No Assamese girl who does not weave can expect to become a wife. And she weaves fairy tales in cloth" (*ibid.*).

Kanaklata Baruah, whose teen-aged heart was bleeding for the country, brought new glory for the Assamese women by dying a noble death in 1942. "Kanaklata was the youngest, yet one of the bravest of the martyrs of India's Freedom Movement" (Dutta 1975: 44). Sixty-year old Bhogeswari Phookanani did not lag behind. Chandraprava Siakiani, Amalprabha Das, Jnanadalata Dowerah, Khagendrapriya Baruah, Puspalata Das and others of the women's wing in the freedom movement devoted themselves silently to fight for the nation (*ibid.* 19).

In the contemporary times, there are a few parliamentarians and legislators and even ministers from among Assamese women.

Besides politics, in other spheres of society also a few Assamese women have achieved high status in their respective fields. Dharmeswari Devi Barooani, Nalinibala Devi are household names as poetesses. There are others too in the spheres of fine arts, and music and of late, in sports. However, such women who have made a mark in various public spheres are still few and far between in Assam.

vi. *Property, ownership and inheritance* :

In traditional outlook, property in the case of an Assamese woman includes generally income, earned by herself, her personal ornaments, clothes, etc. She can consider the garments woven by herself as her private property. A gift made to a daughter at her marriage belongs to her absolutely over which her husband cannot lay claim. Traditionally, the women had no claim to real estate and other immovable property (e.g., the house) belonging either to her father or to her husband. The *dayabhaga* system of inheritance is followed in Assamese society. Sons inherit the father's property after the latter's death. Legally, there has been a change through the provisions of the Hindu Succession Act 1956 (section 10, Rule 4 i), whereby daughters and the widow of the deceased can also inherit shares equal to those of the sons (Desai 1986:964). However, the force of custom still dominates the property inheritance system. Many daughters tend to refrain from claiming their shares. At times many women are also compelled to give up their claims.

vii. *Women in Assamese cultural context* :

Assamese women have occupied an important position in the cultural front of society from time immemorial. Besides attending to various household duties, they have certain specific roles in the social context.

It is generally the house wife who takes a leading role in household level religious activities aimed at ensuing the welfare of her husband, children and other members of the family. It is she who generally observes fast for rituals to be performed. In the absence of a woman it is not possible for a family to celebrate various *Bihus*, which constitute the most important series of festivals of the Assamese people. It is the woman, who offers a *gamocha* (a hand-woven towel) as *bihuwan* (ceremonial *Bihu* gift) to the male members of the household as well as to other relatives and friends during the time of *Rongali Bihu* observed during mid-April. She prepares certain special sweets such as *pitha, laroo,* and other delicacies as a part of the celebration. Feminine participation, specially of unmarried girls, is also a feature of the famous *Rongali Bihu* song and dances of Assam. Young men and women sing and dance together.

Feminine participation in dance is one of the characteristic features of Assamese culture. "Many literary works, particularly the Tantrik works make references to the institution of *devadasis* or temple dancers in the service of the main object of worship, particularly in *Siva* temples" (Choudhury 1987:326).

As Neog (1969:91) points out "The *natis* used to remain unmarried all through life. They, however, lived with their parents and relatives and attended the temple services. With the gradual social deterioration of this class of women dancers, the exit of this dance was complete by the close of the 19th century." Barua (1969:135) also opines that the custom of *devadasis* was prevalent in Assam up to modern period. He referred to the prevalence of virgin worship, *Kumari puja,* once found in Assam.

There are many instances of performance in Assamese folk culture made by women. In some rural areas of lower Assam, there is an institution called *api-oja,* (api—girl, oja—lead singer) singing and dancing are undertaken simultaneously by the *oja.* It is a classical pattern of lyrical recitation and dancing to relate to the audience stories from the *Ramayana, Mahabharata* and *Puranas. Api-oja* performance is generally organised on festive occasions where only womenfolk participate (Bharali 1984:34-35).

Biya-nam (marriage songs), *ai-nam* (songs addressed to presiding deity of pox), *dhainam* (songs relating to birth and delivery), *nisukani-git* (lullby) are some of the folk-songs of Assam with the performance of which women alone are associated (Bardoloi 1983:77-87).

In addition, the womenfolk recite the devotional prayer-songs (*nam*) or read the *'Gita'* in the *namghars* of Assam specially in the months of *Bohag* (April-May) and *Bhada* (August-Sept.). The women also have active roles in the celebration of life crises rites like *annaprasana* (ceremonial giving of first rice meal to infants) and wedding.

viii. *Dress and ornament* :

The Assamese women's attire is highly distinctive. In fact, over the years, the women's dress has come to acquire symbolic significance of Assamese culture as whole. The women wear *mekhela* covering the lower part of the body from waist down to the ankles and *chadar* as a wrap draping the loins over the *mekhela* and also the upper part of the body. Some married women wear an additonal piece of garment for the upper part called *riha. Riha* with its distinctive mode of wearing makes the dress of an Assamese woman graceful. In addition, the blouse has become a part and parcel of Assamese women's attire. The women of rural areas of Assam weave their clothes in traditional design and colour even today in their household looms.

The women of various tribal groups of Assam wear their respective traditional dresses. But some of them wear *mekhela-*

chadar too. Sari is also used by some educated unmarried girls in the present day rural society.

Use of various types of ornaments are common among the womenfolk of Assam. Ornaments of gold and silver are often enough made in traditional designs.

Demographic perspective

Demography is the quantitative study of human populations with strong roots in sociology. It evaluates and initially digests the vast reservoirs of social data compiled in censuses and vital statistics (Encyclopaedia of soc. sc. 1972 : 348).

i. *Number of women and sex-ratio* :

According to 1971 census there are 7,072,478 females in Assam making up 47.3 per cent of the total population. The district of Kamrup (lately divided in Kamrup, Nalbari and Barpeta) has the highest number (1,344,034) of women, while North Cachar Hills district has the lowest number (34,733). The sex-ratio[6] for the whole State (in 1971) is 897. But in the rural areas the ratio is a little more favourable being 913. In the urban areas it is 749. In 1961, the rural sex ratio was 890 while in the urban areas it was 665 (1961 census). In both 1961 and 1971, the urban sex-ratio was lower than in rural one. The lower sex-ratio in the urban areas was due obviously to the fact that there was always a large floating male population in the towns and the conditions of life in urban areas were not suitable for the workers, especially wage labourers, to bring their wives and families.

When we take up another demographic parameter, namely, rural-urban distribution, it is seen that Assam as a whole is among the least urbanised States of India — the percentage of urban residents being only 8.9 of the total population in 1971. When a comparison is made between the two sexes of the State's population, it is found that the women are even more rural than male. Thus while the percentage of urban male in Assam is 57.3, only 42.7 per cent of the women are urban.

ii. *Literacy and education* :

In Assam, the percentage of literacy is around 28 for the whole population (1971 census). Female literacy is much lower (18.6 per

---

[6] Sex-ratio : Number of females per 1000 males.

cent) than in the case for male (36.7 per cent). Among the literate women, the majority (59.3 per cent) are living in the urban areas. Only 20.2 per cent are rural women.

If we look back to the 1951 census, we find a very poor condition of female literacy rate in the rural areas of Assam. Percentage of literate women out of the total rural female population was only 6.6 and in case of urban females it was 37.7 per cent. It indicates a very low literacy level when the total female population (1951 census) consisted of 96 per cent from rural and 4 per cent from the urban areas of the State. However, female literacy in Assam is gradually increasing both in urban and in rural areas.

Table 5 shows that out of the total illiterate persons in 1971, majority (53.5 per cent) are the female population. Among the literates (which include the figures of educational levels are classifiable) table shows only 36.3 per cent of women. As regards female literacy at different educational levels, it is higher at primary level being 33.2 per cent. But from the middle, the female literacy begins to decline. The reason for the decline in the number of women at higher levels of school and education in general is not far to seek. As the girls grow up, they are kept within the home and become progressively engaged in domestic work. After attainment of puberty, the girls in the rural areas are often compelled to leave school. Distance of school and poor economic condition of the parents also prevent them from going to other places for continuing higher studies. Lower age at marriage for girls is still another factor.

Table 5

Literate persons in Assam (1971) according to educational level

	Illiterate	*Literates (without educational level)*	*Educational levels*					
			Primary	*Middle*	*Matriculation or Higher Secondary*	*Non-technical diploma or certificate not equal to degree*	*Technical diploma or cer-tificate not equal to degree*	*Graduate and above*
Persons	10661978	1211103	1609034	829900	271379	9760	4765	60375
Males (%)	46.5	63.7	66.8	96.0	82.3	92.0	96.3	84.5
Females (%)	53.5	36.3	33.2	4.0	17.7	8.0	3.7	15.5

Source : Census of India, 1971, Series 3, part II-C(ii) ; pp. 56-57.

iii. *Age at marriage* :

According to 1971 census, the percentage of Hindu women who were married before attaining 13 years of age is very low in Assam being 9.7 for rural areas and 10.5 for urban areas. Table 6 shows a higher percentage of marriage in the age-group of 13-17. It is 56.3 for rural areas and 54.7 for urban areas.

Table 6

Distribution of currently married (1971) Hindu women in Assam by age at marriage (in percentage)

Age group of the married women	*Rural*	*Urban*
Less than 13 years	9.7	10.5
13-17	56.3	54.7
18-22	28.1	25.3
23-27	2.1	3.0
28 +	0.6	0.6
Unspecified	3.2	5.9

Source : Census of India, 1971, Series 3, Part II-C(ii); pp. 190, 194.

Table 7

Distribution of currently married (1971) women in Assam by age at marriage in relation to educational level (in percentage)

Age Group	*Illiterate*		*Literate but less than Matriculate*		*Matriculate and above*		*Graduate and above*	
	Rural	*Urban*	*Rural*	*Urban*	*Rural*	*Urban*	*Rural*	*Urban*
Less than 13 years	14.2	16.3	8.6	6.4	2.9	1.9	-	1.4
13-17	56.1	56.2	60.5	57.0	36.5	23.0	18.6	9.0
18-22	24.2	18.6	26.0	28.1	46.2	55.6	55.3	48.5
23-27	2.0	1.5	2.0	2.9	9.0	12.2	21.8	31.4
28 +	0.7	0.5	0.4	0.6	0.8	1.3	1.2	4.4
Unspecified	2.8	6.9	2.5	5.0	4.6	6.0	3.1	5.3

Source : Census in India, 1971, Series 3, Part II-C(ii); pp. 204, 206.

It is, however, seen that the rising literacy rate in the State has pushed the marriage age of women upwards. If we analyse the age at marriage by literacy level, high percentage of married women will be found in the higher age-groups.

Table 7 clearly indicates that in the 13-17 age-group the percentage of married illiterates is very high (56 per cent) in both rural and urban areas. Literates with education below matriculation standard also show high percentages of married women being 60.5 and 57.0, respectively for rural and urban areas. But the percentage of married women in this age-group gradully declines as the educational qualification rises to matriculation and upwards.

In the age-group 18-22, there are more married women at nigher literacy level, in both rural and urban areas. In case of graduate women, who got married between 18-22 years, the percentages in rural and urban areas are 55.3 and 48.5, respectively.

A noticeably high percentage of married women is also seen among the graduates who are found to have married after 22 years of age. The percentages of women whose age at marriage was between 23 and 27, are 21.8 in rural areas and 31.4 in urban areas. This shows that the higher the literacy level the higher also is the age of marriage.

iv. *Marital status and emergence of single women* :

The 1971 census provides information regarding age and marital status of the female population of Assam. It is found that 55.5 per cent of the total female population is grouped under 'never married' category. In Table 8, it is seen that in the age-group 10-14, the percentage of 'never married' women is 99.5. It shows near complete absence of child marriage in Assam. The percentage declines to 55.9 in the next age-group namely, 15-19.

The percentage of married female population is 37.2. The number of married females below the age of 9 years is nil. Even in the 10-14 age-group, the percentage of married women is only 0.5. The percentage suddenly rises only from the age group of 15-19. The highest percentage is found in the age group 25-29. This indicates a higher age of marriage now prevailing in society.

The percentage of married females gradually declines in the higher age-groups. The reason for this decline can be explained by widowhood and divorced or separated marital status.

The percentage of widows comes to 6.7. Their percentage is negligible in the age-group 10-14. Widowhood begins in the 15-19 age-group and increases progressively to higher age-groups.

The percentage of divorced or separated women in Assam is very low being only 0.57. The dissolution of marriage by divorce or separation is a new phenomenon in Assam giving rise to a new segment in the category of single women.

Table 8

Distribution of femal population of age and marital status in Assam in 1971 (in percentage)

Age group	*Never Married*	*Married*	*Widowed*	*Others (Divorced separated & unspecified)*
10-14	99.5	0.5	-	-
15-19	55.9	42.9	0.2	1.0
20-24	14.5	83.2	0.9	1.4
25-29	3.6	93.2	1.9	1.3
30-34	1.5	93.1	4.4	1.0
35-39	0.9	90.9	7.3	0.9
40-44	0.8	83.3	14.9	1.0
45-49	0.8	75.9	22.2	1.1
50-54	0.4	65.5	33.0	1.1
55-59	0.4	51.5	46.9	1.2
60 & above	0.4	29.9	68.6	1.1
Age not stated	11.9	74.1	9.1	4.9

Source : Census of India, 1971, Series 3, Part IX; P. 36.

3

GUWAHATI : THE SETTING

The researcher chose Guwahati as the field for her study, because the phenomenon of single women as a category has made its appearance more markedly in this city than in any other place of Assam.

Introduction

Guwahati is situated on the south bank of the mighty river Brahmaputra at an altitude of 55 metres from the sea level, the latitude and longitude being 26°10 45 (N) and 91°45 (E), respectively. Though surrounded by many small hills, the municipal area of the town consists mainly of the plain lands of alluvial origin (Fig. 4).

Guwahati is the temporary capital of Assam as well as the headquarters of the district of Kamrup. But apart from the administrative aspect, its importance lies in its being the centre of trade, commerce, industry, education and culture. Besides, it is the gateway to all the other six States of the North-Eastern region and is connected by road, rail and air with the rest of India. It was connected with the rest of India by the Assam Bengal Railway in 1890. "The importance of the town is proved by the existing remains of temples and fortifications, found in an area extending over miles" (Choudhury 1987 : 436). Numerous temples of different gods and goddesses in and around the city, such as Kamakhya, Umananda, Sukreswar, Baneswar, Ugratara, Navagraha, Chatrakar, Aswaklanta and Manikarneswar have enhanced the beauty of the place.

Historical background of growth and development of the town

Guwahati is a recently modified term from the original 'Gauhati'. It is an anglicised form of the Assamese word 'Gua-hati', meaning the village of areca nut (Saikia compiled 1984 : *Assam-Bandhu* : 365). Guwahati was formerly known as *Pragjotishpura.*

From the historic times, Guwahati has been a prominent centre of many ruling dynasties. During the Ahom period, it became the provincial capial of the Western region of Assam and served as a bulwark against Muslim invasions.

After the British annexation of Assam in 1826, the capital of the province was established in Shillong and not in Guwahati. Even then, the reputation of the town as a centre for trade and commerce remained unchallenged.

Guwahati has been a centre of formal education of Assam and North-East India as a whole for a fairly long time. Western type of education began in a limited way in the mid-nineteenth century following the annexation of Assam by the British. The oldest high school of Guwahati is the Collegiate High School, established in the year 1834. A few other schools were also established in the colonial period. The first college of Assam namely, Cotton College was established in Guwahati in 1901, followed by other institutions of higher learning like the Handique College, established in 1939. Thus a base for formal education was laid down in the town during the pre-Independence period. Following Independence in 1947, the number of educational institutions in the town increased. With the establishment of Guwahati University in 1948 and various other technical institutions, Guwahati became the main educational centre of Assam. According to a survey report conducted by census of India in the early part of 1972, there were 9 nursery schools, 48 primary schools, 31 middle schools, 25 secondary and higher secondary schools, 4 technical schools, 6 colleges and one law college inside the municipal area (census of India 1971:133). During the last few years, the numbers of these institutions have been increased in the greater Guwahati area.

Apart from being an educational centre, Guwahati has assumed considerable importance for the existence of its various administrative and cultural institutions. Among the existing administrative offices, the office of the Deputy Commissioner (established in 1861) and that of the Superintendent of Police (1876) are the oldest. Some other contemporary important offices are office of the Gauhati Municipal Board (1865), the General Post Office (1872) and the Gauhati Railway Station (1890). Other important offices and public buildings established during the present century are Assam State Museum (1940), the Gauhati High Court (1948), the All India Radio (1948), the District Library (1961), the Office of the Town and Country Planning (1969), the Food Corporation of India (1969). After the formation of the State of Meghalaya, many government offices such as the office of the Commissioner of Taxes, State P.W.D., which were previously functioning in Shillong, shifted to Guwahati.

In 1951, this premier city of North-Eastern India had an area of 7.7 sq. kms. The limit of the municipality was extended during the decade and we find an area of 14.24 sq. kms. in 1961 census. After the extension of the municipal area, a large number of commercial and industrial establishments started in and around the town. According to 1971 census, there are 6,525 different establishments in Guwahati. Of these 61 per cent are commercial establishments, 16.2 per cent are industrial establishments and 22.8 per cent are other establishments such as offices, schools, colleges and hospitals.

An important industry in Guwahati is public sector oil refinery set up by Government of India and commissioned in 1960. Some other industrial establishments, mainly in the private sector, are Indian Oxygen Ltd. (established in 1961), The Assam Carbon Products Ltd. (1963), The Assam Industrial Corporation (1969), The Assam Canvas and Craft Industry (1960) and the Hindustan Polythene (1970). A large number of other medium and small manufacturing units dealing with diverse types of products have been established in the different sectors in greater Guwahati area in the recent years.

The capital of Assam was shifted from Shillong to Guwahati in 1973-74. It brought about some remarkable changes in the development and population pattern of the town. Since mid-1970s, the area of the town has grown tremendously because of rural and subrural neighbouring areas of the town being under the jurisdiction of the municipal limits (see Fig. 4). The area of Guwahati has increased to 216.19 sq. kms. in 1981 (Nath 1988:71).

Guwahati was a Class III town till 1951 census and registered as a Class I town in 1961. During the decade from 1961 to 1971 there has been an increase of 23,076 persons in Guwahati. According to 1971 census the population of the city is 123,783. The population increase of twelve large cities (Calcutta, Bombay, Delhi, Bangalore, etc.) has averaged at 40 per cent during 1971-81 while that of Guwahati has registered 182 per cent for the same period (Bhattacharyya ed. 1988 : 94). No census was undertaken in Assam in 1981, but according to an estimate the city's population stands at 4.5 lakhs in 1981, on the strength of which it has been declared recently as a B-2 city (The Assam Tribune, 29 June 1989). The urban population of Guwahati has thus shown tremendous growth in the recent years mostly due to accelerated migration. "A thorough mathematical estimates have shown that the figure would be around 12 lakhs by 2001 A.D. (Bhattacharyya ed. 1988:94).

Population pattern

The composition of population is not only a reflection of its social history but has an indicator of the kinds of social problems that may come in future. Of the 123,783 persons (in 1971) in Guwahati, the percentages of male and female are 61.0 and 39.0, respectively. The density of population of the town is calculated at 8,693 persons per sq. km. in 1971, against 7,072 persons in 1961 and 5,613 persons in 1951 census. Table 9 gives the details of the population growth in the town with the percentage variation from 1901 to 1971.

Table 9
Population Pattern of Guwahati : 1901 - 1971

Year	*Persons*	*Males*	*Females*	*Sex ratio*
1901	11,661	7,772	3,889	500
1911	12,481	8,138	4,343	534
1921	16,480	10,786	5,684	528
1931	21,797	14,506	7,291	503
1941	29,598	18,883	10,715	567
1951	48,615	27,990	15,625	558
1961	100,707	67,289	33,429	497
1971	123,783	75,583	48,200	638

Source : Census of India, 1971, Series 3, Part VI-B, p. 4. (Special survey reports on selected towns—Guwahati.)

The sex-ratio was comparatively higher in 1941 and 1951. It again went down in 1961. The fluctuation is not easy to explain. But the census report of 1971 has opined that the process of industrialization of the town started during the fifties of this century and most of the industrial workers who migrated from outside the town did not bring their families along with them. Gradually it might have been possible for them to solve their accommodation problem and bring their families to the town resulting in slight improvement from 497 in 1961 to 638 in 1971 (Census of India, 1971).

The phenomenal growth of population in the town of Guwahati is mainly due to migration. Table 10.1 shows the distribution of population according to migration status.

According to the place of last residence, the percentages of migrants and non-migrants are 59.3 and 40.7, respectively.

Table 10.1

Distribution of population (1971) in Guwahati according to migration status

	Absolute population			*Percentage distribution*	
	Total population	*Non-Migrant*	*Migrant*	*Nonmigrant*	*Migrant*
Persons	101,474	41,328	60,146	40.7	59.3
Males	61,982	21,558	40,424	34.8	65.2
Females	39,492	10,770	19,722	50.1	49.9

Table 10.2

Distribution of migrants (1971) in Guwahati according to their places of last residence

Last residence	*Migrants*	*Percentage*
1. Different places of Kamrup District (inclusive of present districts of Nalbari and Barpeta)	17,329	28.8
2. Different districts of the State	15,327	25.5
3. Different States of India	17,176	28.6
4. From other countries	10,314	17.1

Source : Census of India, 1971, Series 3, Part VI-B, p. 79
(Special survey reports on selected towns—Guwahati.)

Table 10.2 shows that the percentage of migrants from different places of Kamrup district is the highest, being 28.8. Those born in Sibsagar district and enumerated in Guwahati come next, followed by persons born in the districts of Nagaon, Goalpara, Cachar, Darrang, Lakhimpur, Mikir Hills and North Cachar Hills but enumerated in Guwahati.

Improved communication has contributed to the flow of migration. All the important towns, districts and sub-divisional headquarters of the State are now well-connected with Guwahati by rail, road and air. It is also connected with almost all the places of Kamrup by road. Spectacular development of roadways connecting Guwahati with its rural hinterland and most other places of Assam and North East India has led to rapid growth of truck and bus traffic. Motor buses play a significant role, both in terms of intra-city and inter-locality movements.

The statement below shows the percentage of female migrants to Guwahati from the various districts :

District of birth	*Percentage of the female migrants*
1. Goalpara	16.5
2. Darrang	13.3
3. Nagaon	19.3
4. Sibsagar	23.2
5. Lakhimpur	13.1
6. Mikir Hills	0.7
7. N.C. Hills	0.9
8. Cachar	13.0

Source : Census of India, 1971 Series 3, Part VI-B, p. 79
(Special survey reports on selected towns—Guwahati.)

Social profile of the city

According to 1971 census, there are 11 languages spoken by different sections of the people in the town as their mother-tongue. Among them the number of Assamese speaking persons is highest (47.25 per cent of the total population). They are followed by persons speaking Bengali (18.5%), Bihari (18%), Manipuri (7.44%), Telugu (4.83%), Marwari (4.23%), Bodo (3.96%), Nepali (2.61%), Punjabi (1.94%), Rajasthani (0.60%) and Hindi (0.47%) languages.

The Hindus constitute the numerically dominant religious

community in Guwahati accounting for nearly 87 per cent of the town's population in 1971. The Muslims are the next largest group (9.9 per cent). The remainder of the townmen variously profess Sikhism, Christianity, Jainism, Buddhism and other religions (1971 census).

The census does not provide figures for various Hindu caste groups, except for the scheduled caste inhabitants of Guwahati. The scheduled castes of the city include the Kaibartta, Bansphor, Bania, Namasudra and other minor groups representing 4.5 per cent of the total population of the city. The caste Hindu population comprises the Brahmins, Kayasthas, Kalitas, Ahoms and other minor groups. There are also a few scheduled tribe communities in Guwahati like Bodo Kacharis, the Sonowal Kacharis, Lalung, Mech and Rabha. They constitute 1.7 per cent of the Guwahati population (*ibid.*).

Literate persons constitute 64.5 per cent and illiterate 35.5 per cent of Guwahati population. In all age-groups, male-literacy is higher than female. Among females, the highest literacy rate is in the age-group of 15-19, followed by the age-groups of 20-24, 10-14, 25-34, 5-9 and 35 + (*ibid.*)

Age at marriage of educated women (as per 1971 census) is higher than that of illiterate women. From the Table 11 it is found that 17.6 per cent of the illiterate women got married before the age of 13 years. Among the literate women on the other hand, those who got married before the age of 13 years form only 6.5 per cent. It is further found that 50.9 per cent of the women having education up to matriculation standard got married at the age of 18 to 22 years. Those who went up to graduation level or above got married between the ages of 23 and 27 years. Their percentage is 46.0.

Table 11

Age at marriage of currently married (1971) women of Guwahati according to educational level

Age at marriage	*Educational level*			
	Illiterates	*Literates up to Matriculation standard*	*Matriculate and above but less than graduates*	*Graduates and above*
Less than 13 years	17.6	6.5	2.2	2.7
13-17 yrs.	53.6	54.5	23.5	8.2
18-22 yrs.	13.4	27.4	50.9	19.7
23-27 yrs.	2.1	3.4	12.8	46.0
28 +	0.6	0.5	2.3	3.5
Age not stated	12.7	7.7	8.3	19.9

Source : Census of India 1971, Series 3, Part VI-B, p. 52 (Special survey reports on selected towns — Guwahati).

The social complexion of this old established town of Assam at present is far from homogeneous. There are many discrete social and ethnic categories among its residents and they too are not bound by the dictates of their age-old traditions and customs. The city as a whole cannot be conceived as a unified social field. Among the many socio-ethnic categories a changing modes of life are also becoming more and more marked.

The process of urbanization has changed the social behaviour of the various groups of people. As a result, the traditional joint families found among many communities of Guwahati are breaking up into nuclear families. Nuclear family-centred households are becoming a common feature in the realm of family organisation in the city.

It is revealed in the census (1971) that in the family composition of the mixed society of Guwahati, most of the households have male heads. It reflects an overall patriarchal pattern of society. Where, however, the male is away from the place of residence for reasons of service elsewhere or where the marriage has been dissolved either by death or by divorce, the female members of the household are found to shoulder the burden of the family.

Emergence of single women

Though, traditionally, Assamese women were freer than their counterparts in some other parts of India, they were not encouraged to go out seeking jobs. But in the existing urban society, a deviation from this age-old custom is noticed in many Assamese households of the city. Women are found to be increasingly engaged in the pursuit of education and in salaried jobs. This has resulted in the rise of age at marriage as well as a rise in the number of unmarried (or never married) women.

Out of the total 58,082 'never married' persons of Guwahati (calculated from 80% non-sample slips of 1971 census), 36,568 are males and as many as 21,514 are females. The percentage of 'never married' females is matched against respective age-groups as follows :

Age group	*Percentage of never married women*
15-19	65.2
20-24	30.3
25-29	6.8
30-34	2.7

From the above figures, it is evident that early marriage for girls is not very much in vogue in Guwahati.

The percentage of widowed males and females to the total male and female persons are 0.88 and 3.79, respectively. The percentage is thus comparatively lower in the case of the widowed males. The reason is that most of the widowed males get remarried after their wives' death. But the case is not the same with the females. Barring few enlightened persons, widow remarriage is not yet very common, mainly because of the continuing stigma attached to it.

In the 1971 census, 89 divorced or separated persons are recorded in Guwahati. Among them, 23 are males and 66 females. In the case of females the highest number of divorce cases are found in the age group 25-29.

From the above account it is apparent that rapid urban growth, accompanied by immigration, has led to the emergence of a fair number of 'single women' in Guwahati. The city thus offers a suitable setting for investigating this newly emerged phenomenon. Here the educational and occupational opportunities for such a type of women are more than in other small urban locales of Assam. The city of Guwahati offers all kinds of educational facilities from the pre-primary schools to the university. Institutions for acquiring technical and semi-technical skills, handicarft training, weaving, etc., are also there. In addition, as will be evident later, there are special institutional facilities to cater to the needs and problems of single women, for example, the State Home for Destitute Women, Kasturba Ashram and working women's hostel.

In the occupational sphere also Guwahati offers more scope than other urban areas of the State. From the 1971 census, it has been found that the highest participation rate of female workers is in different services being 10.7 per cent out of the total working population in this category. In the household industry, the percentage of female workers is slightly high being 12.6. The main activities under this category are the production of broomsticks, can and bamboo baskets, hand-loom clothes and toys.

In the sourthern part of the city there is an industrial belt in which hardware, food processing plants and some workshops are situated. In the eastern part also there is an industrial estate where various production centres are located, providing occupational opportunities even to the illiterate Assamese women.

Rapid expansion of the city has converted many suburban and rural areas into fully urbanized areas in the recent years. Traditional customs in these areas in the ways of living have experienced change under the impact of modernity. In these areas, it is no longer considered improper for a woman to accept work for earning livelihood. The rise in the cost of standard of living has compelled even the middle-class families, who generally stick to their traditions more rigidly than others, to allow their womenfolk to work outside domestic arena.

This trend of women working outside the domestic arena has been aided by commuting facilities in Guwahati. In addition to city bus services, almost every villlage of Kamrup district is within easy reach of the city by public bus service. Many women from neighbouring villages of Guwahati can come in the morning and go back in the evening, after working in different establishments in Guwahati.

These facilities are not available in most other urban or semi-urban areas of Assam. There are industrial towns like Digboi, Duliajan and Namrup. These towns have by and large remained like 'closed' towns for single women as they lack many support-facilities in small towns.

PART TWO

PROFILES OF THE SINGLE WOMEN

4

SOCIAL BACKGROUND OF THE SINGLE WOMEN

Social background of the respondents is an important variable in any social research. As Kaur (1983 : 18) observes : "It will enable us to understand clearly the diverse factors affecting the value-orientation of the respondents, their age, sex and caste, their educational standard, economic status, occupation, etc." An attempt has been made, therefore, to provide background material on the women in the sample.

Marital status

Marriage confers a special status and identity to women in the Assamese society. The structure and functions of a family change with the alteration of marital status of individuals in it.

Since this study is concerned exclusively with single women, the sample consists of women who are widows, divorcees[7] and who have never entered into matrimony. Table 4 shows that 40 single women in the sample were married, but became widows; 30

[7] Unless specified, the term 'divorcee' in the context of this study includes women who are not legally separated from husband but lives separately.

were married, but separated from husbands by divorce and informal separation and 40 remained unmarried. The sample thus represents more or less or even mix of the different categories of single women stratified according to marital status.

In this and the subsequent chapters, the material has been arranged on the basis of marital status of single women as widow, divorcee and unmarried. The widows are discussed first as their current marital status is confirmed by the death of husband. The marital status of the divorced and separated women is not as distinct as the widows. Hence, they are discussed after the widows. The unmarried women have a probability of marriage. Because of the uncertainity of their current marital status, they are discussed in the third place.

Age structure

The marital maturity and physical capabilities of a woman are dependant on her age. The social responsibilities, obligation and, to a great extent, the role of a woman are also linked up with her age. Hence, age can be considered as a major contributing factor of social background of the women in the sample.

Table 12 shows that 21.8 per cent of single women of all categories come from the age group of 30-34 and another 20 per cent from the age group of 35-39. Thus, a little more than 40 per cent of the women are in the 30-39 age group. This is a matter of great social significance. A considerable number of women acquired the single status at the peak of their lives. This enforced on them a new role to which they were required to adjust. These women, at the time of study, are continuing in their single lives. The children of the widows and divorcees are also so young that they are not in a position to help their mothers.

Table 12
Age distribution of single women in the sample

Age group	*Widow*	*Divorcee*	*Unmarried*	*Total*	
				Number	*Per cent*
a	*b*	*c*	*d*	*e*	*f*
15-19	-	1	-	1	0.9
20-24	1	5	-	6	5.5
25-29	6	4	-	10	9.1
30-34	7	5	12	24	21.8

a	*b*	*c*	*d*	*e*	*f*
35-39	9	6	7	22	20.0
40-44	4	1	7	12	10.9
45-49	7	3	4	14	12.7
50-54	3	5	2	10	9.1
55-59	2	-	6	8	7.3
60 & above	1	-	2	3	2.7
	40	30	40	110	100.0

To come to each category in turn : So far as the widows are concerned their number gradually rises from the age group of 20-24 till the peak is reached at the age group of 35-39. It then gradually peters off to the lowest number at the age of 60 and above.

As regards the second category of single women, namely, divorcees, the figures for age-group do not exhibit a definite pattern like those of widows or unmarried women. As the table shows, there is no consistent pattern in the distribution of divorcees in different age-groups.

So far as unmarried women are concerned, it has already been stated (Chapter 1) that women below 30 years are excluded from the sample as they have the possibility of marriage. Of the women above 30 years, the largest concentration is found in the 30-34 age-group. It may be assumed that some of them still have the possibility of marriage. The number gradually tapers off with the rise of the age, except in the 55-59 age-group. The reason for this exception may be due to the fact that at this age, women finally and definitely settle down in their unmarried status. Except for this exceptional group, the number of unmarried women gradually goes down as the age of the women increases (Fig. 5).

Education level

Educational attainment of a woman plays an important part in determining her standard of living, socio-cultural status and esteem accorded her by the society. Educational attainment influences her outlook, attitudes and capacity for adjustment to myriad demands of her circumstances. Educational status can, therefore, be considered as an useful index to socio-economic position of an individual. The sample covers both literate and illiterate women (Fig. 6).

Table 13

Educational levels of women in the sample

Educational level	*Widow*	*Divorcee*	*Unmarried*	*Total*	
				Number	*Per cent*
Primary	4	3	-	7	6.4
Middle-school	4	4	3	11	10.0
Matriculation	4	6	12	22	20.0
Higher Secondary / Pre-University	4	2	5	11	10.0
Graduation	7	4	7	18	16.3
Post-graduation and above	7	4	8	19	17.3
Total Literates	30	23	35	88	80.0
Total Illiterates	10	7	5	22	20.0
Grand Total	40	30	40	110	100.0

In this essentially urban and purposive sample of 110 single women, there is a concentration (80 per cent) of literate and educated women. Table 13 brings out that as many of 88 women had education from primary to post-graduate level. In fact, as many 37 (33.6 per cent) out of 88 educated women were graduates or post-graduates. The preponderance of women with higher educational attainments is because of identification of the sample for study coinciding with working women many of whom are teachers.

Occupational status

Occupation is another important indicator of socio-economic status. The various occupations in which the single women in the sample are involved provide us with an idea of their adjustment to the urban setting of Guwahati as well as their economic status.

Table 14

Occupations of single women in the sample

Occupations	*Widow*	*Divorcee*	*Unmarried*	*Total*	
				Number	*Per cent*
a	*b*	*c*	*d*	*e*	*f*
Teaching:					
i. Primary and Middle school	3	4	3	10	9.1

a	*b*	*c*	*d*	*e*	*f*
ii. Secondary school	3	4	4	11	10.0
iii. College and University	1	2	4	7	6.4
Administrative jobs	1	-	4	5	4.5
Professional service :					
i. Doctor, nurse	2	-	1	3	2.7
ii. Engineer	-	1	1	2	1.8
iii. Lawyer	1	-	2	3	2.7
Clerical jobs	11	2	7	20	18.2
Office attendants	9	-	-	9	8.2
Skilled labour	6	10	7	23	21.0
Social worker	-	-	2	2	1.8
Unemployed inmates of destitute homes	3	7	5	15	13.6
	40	30	40	110	100.0

The occupational distribution of women in various categories indicated in Table 14 yields some interesting information. It is seen that the highest number (28), making up a little more than 25 per cent of the sample, are teachers in different types of educational institutions. The concentration of women in teaching reflects both opportunities available to women as well as their preference for this vocation. In the contemporary Assamese society, teaching is regarded as a 'just' occupation for women and it also carries with it the age-old notion of being a 'noble' profession. However, its income potential has always been limited. Moreover, teaching permits a woman comparatively more time for her household duties because of limited hours of work and vacations.

In the white collar category, there is a higher concentration (18.2 per cent) of women in clerical jobs, such as office assistant, typist, telephone operator, hostel matron and receptionist.

Respondents, working as office attendants (i.e., peon and *ayah*) form 8.2 per cent of the sample. They include both literate and illiterate women. Generally the widows of deceased peons are employed as female peons in the same establishment on compassionate ground.

The skilled labour category (21 per cent of the sample) includes 9 weavers and 7 polythene bag-makers working in different organizations of the city. Weaving is a traditional female occupation in the Assamese society. In the city, women weavers are also working in small-scale production centres using power looms.

Polythene bag making is an occupation offering opportunity of employment to women who have no education. Women are employed to make bags on wage or contract basis. There is one woman who works in a beauty parlour for women as hair dresser. Five other women are working as either cooks or cleaners in different establishments. Another woman works in a factory in the industrial estate which manufactures car and floor polish.

Social work, particularly in the context of women, is a newly emergent field in Assam attracting many women workers. There are two such social workers in the sample, one of them is an unmarried who has general education up to B.A. level and additional training as a social worker. She works as a secretary in the local Women's Welfare Organization. The other (also an unmarried woman) is a matriculate and works in the same organization.

It is seen that 15 (13.6 per cent) women are lodged at destitute homes for want of suitable employment and place of living. They are engaged in sweeping and cleaning the establishments, cooking food for the inmates and receiving training in making toys, leather bags and children's garments. Though some of them have education, they are not employed in any other way.

Income

The level of earning is an important aspect of social background. It also determines the socio-economic status of an individual. Table 15 shows the monthly income of the women in the sample. The women living in the destitute homes have no cash income. They are supported and maintained by the homes.

Table 15
Income levels of single women in the sample

Monthly income range (in rupees)	*Widow*	*Divorcee*	*Unmarried*	*Total*	
				Number	*Per cent*
a	*b*	*c*	*d*	*e*	*f*
Up to 200	7	10	9	26	23.6

a	*b*	*c*	*d*	*e*	*f*
200-400	2	2	-	4	3.6
401-600	13	-	-	13	11.8
601-800	6	5	8	19	17.3
801-1000	3	3	6	12	11.0
1001-1200	1	2	6	9	8.2
1201-1400	2	-	1	3	2.7
1401-1600	-	1	2	3	2.7
1601-Above	3	-	3	6	5.5
Income not stated	3	7	5	15	13.6
	40	30	40	110	100.0

Monthly income of the remaining women have been shown in 9 different slabs. These slabs may be grouped into three broad categories — lower, middle and higher. The lower income group consists of income-range up to Rs. 600.00, the middle from Rs. 601.00 to 1200.00 and the higher from Rs. 1201.00 to 1601.00 and above.

The lower income group makes up 39 per cent, the middle income group 36.5 per cent and the higher income group only 10.9 per cent of the sample. Taking the destitutes together with the women in the lower income group, it is seen that more than 52 per cent of the women are hard pressed to procure even the minimum requirements of food, clothes and shelter (Fig. 7).

Place of origin and migration

The women in the sample show considerable diversity in terms of their place of origin. The sample consists of a *mixed population derived* from rural, semi-urban and urban areas of Assam having different types of soico-economic bankground (Fig. 8).

Table 16.1
Migration status of single women in the sample

	Migrants	*Local*	*Total*
Widow	24	16	40
Divorcee	22	8	30
Umarried	18	22	40
	64	46	110
Percentage (to the total 110)	58.2	41.8	

Table 16.1, 16.2 and 16.3 provide the picture of place of origin and migration of the 110 women in the sample. Not all the women originally belonged to Guwahati. In fact, the majority (58.2 per cent) are migrants to the city (Table 16.1). Of the 64 migrants, the widows are more in number constituting 37.5 per cent. Next to them, the divorced women make up 34.4 per cent of the migrants and the unmarried 28.1 per cent.

Table 16.2
Migration streams of single women in the sample

	Urban to urban	*Rural to urban*	*Total*
Widow	4	20	24
Divorcee	6	16	22
Unmarried	7	11	18
	17	47	64
Percentage (to the total 64)	26.6	73.4	

Of the migrants, the largest number (73.4 per cent) of the respondents have come from rural areas (Table 16.2), while remainder (26.6 per cent) have come from other towns of Assam. Among the migrants from rural areas, the widows dominate (about 42.5 per cent) while the unmarried category is the smallest (23.4 per cent).

Table 16.3
Place of origin (District[8]) of single women in the sample

District	*Single women*	
	Number	*Per cent*
i. Goalpara	1	1.6
ii. Kamrup	41	64.0
iii. Darrang	3	4.6
iv. Nagaon	2	3.1
v. Sibsagar	12	19.0
vi. Dibrugarh	3	4.6
vii. Lakhimpur	2	3.1
	64	100.0

[8]District Kamrup is inclusive of Nalbari and Barpeta; Darrang is inclusive of Sonitpur; Sibsagar is inclusive of Golaghat and Jorhat; Goalpara is inclusive of Goalpura and Dhubri.

The single women have to come to Guwahati from villages and towns of different districts of Brahmaputra valley (Table 16.3). But the largest number (64 per cent) is from the undivided district of Kamrup. This is only natural since Guwahati is located in Kamrup district.

Caste composition

A Hindu is known by his or her caste. The caste affiliations of the single women are shown in Table 17.

Table 17
Caste affiliation of single women in the sample

Castes	*Widows*	*Divorcee*	*Unmarried*	*Total*	
				Number	*Per cent*
i. Brahmin	8	10	5	23	21.0
ii. Kayastha	5	5	10	20	18.2
iii. Kalita	9	9	13	31	28.2
iv. Ahom	1	2	-	3	2.7
v. Rajbanshi	1	1	1	3	2.7
vi. Nath	1	1	1	3	2.7
Scheduled castes :					
vii. Kaibartta	12	2	6	20	18.2
viii. Bania	1	-	3	4	3.6
ix. Namasudra	2	-	1	3	2.7
	40	30	40	110	100.0

Table 17 shows that the women belong to as many as nine castes. Of the 110 women, there are more from the Kalita caste followed by Brahmin and Kayastha. There are very few women from castes such as Ahom, Rajbanshi and Nath. The women of the various scheduled castes together constitute nearly a quarter (24.5 per cent) of the single women in the sample. According to 1971 census scheduled castes form 4.5 per cent of the total population of Guwahati and the scheduled tribes form only 1.7 per cent of the city's population. As in other parts of India, the Brahmins have a high ritual status in Assam. Two other castes, namely, the Kayastha and the Kalita, also have high status in the caste hierarchy of Assam. The women from these higher castes make up as much as 67.4 per cent of the sample. This would more or less correspond to the proportion of higher castes group of the city's population.

5

SINGLE STATUS THROUGH WIDOWHOOD

Sati, the practice of immolating in the burning pyre of the deceased husband by the widowed wife, was prohibited in British India in 1829. Though it continued to linger in other parts of India for many years, Assam has been free from this evil practice, as mentioned in Chapter 2. It was a rare phenomenon in Assam (Sarma 1981 : 121).

Describing the position of the widow after prohibition of *sati,* Altekar says :

> "How then were they expected to lead their remaining life? There were three courses open to them. They could either pass their remaining life in widowhood, or have some children by levirate (*niyoga*), or remarry regularly. The first was of course the most honourable course, but there were many who followed the second or the third alternative" (1978 : 143).

It may be mentioned that the custom of levirate was quite uncommon in Assam. Widow remarriage was also a problem. Though Gunabhiram Barua, a literary stalwart of Assam, set an example by remarrying a widow in the 19th century, it was unacceptable in the traditional Assamese Hindu society. Pointing out the case of Gunabhiram Barua, Sarma (1981:115) says that "Sporadic cases of widow remarriage continued, but society did not accept it as an usual phenomenon". It is thus clear that in the Assamese society women had to pass their life in widowhood following the death of husband since long. In her study of the Assamese society, Cantlie (1984:108) also notes that "If she is unfortunate enough to become a widow, she should live a life of pious seclusion wearing no ornaments and eating only cooling foods".

In comparison to the two other categories of single women (i.e., divorcee and unmarried women), it can be said that widowhood is the commonest cause for a woman becoming single in the Assamese Hindu society. An attempt is made below to outline and analyse the cases of widows in contemporary Assamese Hindu society and how they are pushed into the status of single women.

The death of the husband

Of the 40 widows in the sample, as many as 32 (80 per cent) lost their husbands through death by illness. Four husbands died by accident, three by murder, and one by suicide. As reported by the respondents, the diseases were cancer, typhoid, dysentry, gastric-ulcer, tuberculosis or heart-attack. In several cases the diseases were not properly diagnosed and there was little or no treatment.

Age of the women at husbands' death

Because of the increasing age at marriage in the contemporary Assamese society, the proportion of widows of tender age is very small. In table 18 a small number (6) of widows is seen in the age range of 20 years and below. The widows of very tender age (15 years and below) are all Brahmin by caste, among whom child marriage was a customary practice.

Table 18

Age group of the widows in the time of husbands' death

Age group	*Widows*	
	Number	*Per cent*
a	*b*	*c*
15 & below	3	7.5

a	*b*	*c*
16-20	3	7.5
21-25	13	32.5
26-30	9	22.5
31-35	7	17.5
36-40	3	7.5
41-45	2	5.0
	40	100.0

Widowhood thus occurred at a tender age in these few cases. The highest number (29) of women became widow between 21 and 35 years of age — the most important period in a woman's life. Though widowhood at a tender age is unfortunate, it keeps open the possibility of remarriage as well as opportunities for securing employment, or pursuing further studies. This is particularly so, if they are childless. In addition, there are greater prospects of care and support from close kin, such as parents and siblings, in the case of a very young widow. On the other hand, a woman widowed at a more mature age of 30 or more, finds herself without close kin support. Her parents may be old or they may no longer be there. Her brothers might also become more responsible to their respective households and unwilling or unable to give her the required support.

Duration of married life

Duration of a married life has no impact on the life of a woman. A short or long period of married life may change the entire life pattern of the widow. Depending on the duration of her conjugal life, she may think of marrying again or lead a single life. A brief married life signifies the young age of a widow. In the contemporary urban Assamese society, there is a general atmosphere of permissiveness for remarriage of such young widows. On the other hand, a long married life implies that the woman is well past the marriageable age. A long married life could mean that the widow has children and this increases her responsibility towards the children which does not permit her to think of remarriage. Moreover, she is more experienced by the long married life to stand in society alone. A woman having a medium duration of married life has more problem to adjust in her single life as a widow. She usually cannot think of remarriage nor is she be able to cope adequately with single life.

In table 19 the duration of married life is shown in 4 groups, namely, very short duration (below 2 years), short duration (between 2 and 5 years), medium duration (between 5 and 15 years) and long duration (above 15 years).

Table 19
Duration of married life of the widows in the sample

Duration of married life	*Widows*	
	Number	*Per cent*
Very short	8	20.0
Short	9	22.5
Medium	17	42.5
Long	6	15.0
	40	100.0

Table 19 shows that only 6 widows in the sample have had a long married life, i.e., above 15 years. Maikon has had the longest duration of married life, namely, 26 years. She has seven children,— the largest number among the widows in the sample.

Medium duration of married life dominates the sample, 17 widows have had a married life of 5 to 15 years. Widows like Dipika, Subhasini, Taramai had a medium duration of married life.

The number of widows who had short and very short durations of conjugal life are 9 and 8, respectively. Pankaj, Bharati, Rina have had short married lives. The shortest duration was that of Hemalata who belonged to a Brahman family. Her husband dies 15 days after the marriage. She had been married at the age of twelve.

Of the others who had very short married life, Bijaya's husband died after thirty-four days of marriage. Purnima became a widow after four months and Sashi and Kalyani after six months of marriage. Ranjana had a married life for eight months while Dipti and Indira of approximately 2 years.

Relationship with deceased husband's family

The patterns of behaviour between the widow and her affinal kin usually begin to change soon after her widowhood. Such changes are found in nearly all the cases in the sample. The main causes behind the change are as follows :

i. Previously, the woman's husband had been the indirect

> controlling agent of kin relationships between his wife and other members of his family. But the husband's death removes this intermediate and mediating role from the kinship network and increases the direct authority of the deceased's kin over the widow.

After the husband's death, a degradation is seen in the status of a woman in the male dominated Assamese society. In the absence of her husband, she is unable to stand and face life on her own in the family as well as in society. During the life time of her husband, she generally gets the social and economical security provided by the social structure itself. But after her husband's death, she often does not get decent treatment and compassionate understanding of her problems from her affines in the family. Her position begins to degrade and become insecure after the bereavement.

> Kalyani, the daughter of a lawyer of high Kayastha caste had an arranged marriage while she was studying in the college for her B.A. degree. The husband was an engineer belonging to a respectable family of the same caste. The two families hailed from different towns of Upper Assam. Her husband died after six months of the marriage. She thus became a widow at the tender age of twenty. Narrating the facts about her short married life, Kalyani reported:"He died of kidney ailment. He was hospitalized for about four months and we thus lived together for only two months. I could know of his grave illness from the doctor and was therefore mentally prepared for the worst. But I did not anticipate that I will be ill-treated by the members of my husband's family after his death. My mother-in-law labelled me as 'inauspicious' and blamed me for the death of her son".

The premature death of a son, during the life time of his parents, is generally regarded as an unnatural death. There is a superstition that the wife is inauspicious, being under the spell of some star, and thus causing the death of her husband. Such a notion is widely prevalent in Assam. This sort of superstition generates an uncongenial attitude towards the widow and instead of compassion and sympathy she receives hostility and harsh treatment from members of her husband's family. To quote Kalyani further:

> "After the dead body was carried away for cremation,

a new white *dhoti* without border was given to me to wear by my husband's younger sister. She also asked me not to wear any silk clothes. Plain, simple cotton *dhoti* was to be my attire. She removed all my ornaments instead of sympathizing with me. Besides, various restrictions were imposed on me to be followed during the period of mourning. It was quite cold in the month of January. As I had to sleep on the floor, I felt very cold in the night. After two days I became ill and with acute tonsilitis. So my mother discussed the matter with my mother-in-law requesting her to give permission so that I can sleep on bed till my recovery. But this request was refused. Though I knew that those are the customs to be followed by an Assamese Hindu widow, I could not tolerate such strictness as I was ill. I could not adjust to the situation. On the fifteenth day after solemnizing the *sraddha*[9] ceremony, I accompanied my mother to stay in my parents' house and did not ever return to my husband's family".

ii. The breaking away from the joint family of the husband for seeking special avenues after widowhood causes change in the pattern of relationship between the widow and her affinal kin. This change on the one, deprives the widow of shelter, safety and security and on the other, makes her free to seek her own avenues for employment along with her living arrangement.

Bijaya, daughter of a *satradhikar*[10], was married in 1980, interrupting her college study. Her husband was an Instructor in a Junior Technical School in Upper Assam. He had two other brothers and two sisters in the family. All of them lived jointly with their aged parents. Her husband died after a brief illness after only one month and four days of their marriage. It was a great shock to Bijaya. After the death of her husband and after the performance of post-funeral rites by the deceased's brothers, Bijaya began to feel herself as an outsider in the family. Revealing her experiences after widowhood, she said : "I was being treated as an outcast, because I had become a widow. Instead of sympathizing with me, my mother-in-law

---

[9] Sraddha : Funeral rites at the end of death pollution period.

[10] Satradhikar : Head of a *Satra* institution.

cursed me for being responsible for her son's untimely death. She often called me a very inauspicious woman. As I was treated very harshly by my mother-in-law, some of my relatives advised me to find out a way to make myself independent. They also suggested to me to go back to my mother's house. According to them, I could get a chance there to start a new life by entering into remarriage".

Bijaya stayed at her deceased husband's house for three months. When she informed, her elder brother came and took her to his place. He came immediately and with the permission of Bijaya's parents-in-law, she went to her brother's house (at Jorhat) in search of a job.

Bijaya took a three-month typing course staying with her brother. After duly qualifying herself as a typist, she returned to her husband's house to inform them about her resolve to do a job. Later on, she got herself employed in 1981 in a technical institution in Guwahati. She found accommodation in the women's hostel of the institution. She is now leading her single life in Guwahati.

When asked about her relationship with her husband's family members after taking up the job, she said:"After I took up the job, I visited my in-laws' house three times, and I am still trying to maintain cordial relations with that family. But the relationship became very unpleasant when I took the provident fund amount of Rs. 5000.00 of my deceased to which I was entitled. I have, therefore, given up my claim over life insurance amount of Rs. 12,000.00 of my husband in favour of my father-in-law. Another amount of Rs. 3,000.00 which I got as the arrear salary of my husband, I gave away to his younger brother. All this was in an attempt to maintain cordial relations with them".

iii. In case of widows without any issue, then childlessness causes a cooling in the ardour of affection among her affines. A child is a cementing factor is the kinship bond; widow and her affines, in the absence of a child, tend to loosen this bond.

It is seen that usually the parents-in-law want to keep a relation with their widowed daughter-in-law only through the affection they have for their grand-children. Moreover, they tend to see in a grand-child a substitute of their deceased son.

> Kuntala, a widowed mother of two children, stays in residential quarters provided by her employers. Her mother-in-law comes occasionally from her village to see the grand-children.

> Ranjana, who had a posthumous son, lives with her parents. But she is maintaining links with her deceased husband's family through her child. She said : "During *Bihu* or *Puja* holiday or in summer vocation, I try to visit my husband's place at Sibsagar along with my son. My mother-in-law has great affection for him and wants to see him at least once a year". Anima and Bharati also reported in the same way about their relationship with their affinal kin.

Children thus provide a bridge to maintain the ties between a widow and her affinal kin.

The childness widows on the other hand, do not usually maintain such a relationship with their in-laws. Mallika, Dipti, Bijaya, Kalyani are all childless widows. They left their respective deceased husband's place without any difficulties and had no such relationship with the husband's family.

iv. In many families, particularly among the poor, the apprehension that the other members would have to maintain the widow out of their meagre income leads towards stiffening of their attitude towards the widow.

> Subhadra's case can be cited here. Her husband was a *Mahari* (account keeper) in a Marwari shop in Guwahati where they lived. It was a joint household where Subhadra's husband, husband's elder brother with his wife and children, and her aged parents-in-law lived together. Her husband died three and a half years after marriage leaving her behind with a nine-month-old baby. Besides the harsh behaviour of her mother-in-law, the husband's brother also refused to maintain her. Subhadra could not ask them even for the maintenance of her little child. So after about four months, her father took her and the baby away to his house.

In the rural areas of Assam, the affinal kins are found to be a little more considerate and sympathetic towards widows. But the overall attitude towards maintaining a widow by the members of the deceased's famly is the same as in the urban areas.

> Jaymati was living in a village of lower Assam in her husband's joint family. The family consisted of her husband's elder brother, younger brother, one unmarried younger sister and aged parents. All the three brothers, including her husband, were cultivating jointly the family land. As Jaymati reported, her parents-in-law did not like to keep her along with them after her husband's death. Her brother-in-law also did not want to give any maintenance towards her and her children. It became a problem for Jaymati to get even washing soap, medicines, kerosene oil, etc., since she has no income of her own. She could not reconcile herself to stay with them along with her two children. Her only brother was too poor to maintain her. She ultimately decided to leave the village in search of her livelihood. Being informed by some of the villagers about a home for destitute women in Guwahati, she left her husband's house with her little children to take shelter in the home.

v. A rational outlook on the part of the widow herself to stand up and face life on her own, helps her to move out of the deceased husband's family. Most of the widows do not like to be a burden to the members of their husband's family. This outlook changes the pattern of behaviour and relationship between a widow and her husband's family.

Besides, the urban-industrial society has become excessively individualistic so that there is a general tendency for each man to look after himself and his own wife and children only. The changed socio-economic situation is responsible in some cases for loosening the family bond between the widow and her husband's family members.

Some other circumstances in the life of a widow

It is found that widows often have to leave their deceased husband's home and seek employment elsewhere due to circumstance other than the changed behaviour attitude of affines. Some such circumstances are as follows :

When the kin of a widow, whether affinal or consanguineal, are very poor, it is difficult for them to take her responsibility with or without children.

In Assam, the rual people are mostly poor agriculturists. The average land holdings are small and the yields are also lower than all India averages[11]. Poverty forces some of the widows to seek employment elsewhere to adopt a single status.

> Besanti was a posthumous child of her widowed mother. She had one elder sister only. Her father died before her birth and so the family was sheltered by her mother's elder brother. Her mother also died when Basanti was only two years old. Therefore in the absence of their parents, they could not get any education and were given in marriage by their poor maternal uncle just after they attained puberty.
>
> Basanti's husband was working in Guwahati as a clerk in the Railway Department. They had two children and were living in a nearby village on the west of the city. It was a joint household.
>
> After about twenty years of their marriage, her husband died. On her husband's death, as she reported, the members of her husband's family were very much sympathetic towards her, but they were unable to maintain her along with her children. Her husband's brothers were poor cultivators who could not afford to maintain her and her children. They, however, helped her in withdrawing her deceased husband's various dues from his office. One of her husband's younger brothers helped Basanti in finding job in her husband's office. As Basanti had no education she had to join as peon. She then left her husband's native home with the permission of the family to live in the city.
>
> Sarala, another widow, did not have any near kin in

[11]In Assam (1971 Census), the dependence on agriculture is 77.7% against the all India average of 72.6%.

her husband's family. She was married to a man employed as a security guard as Gauhati Refinery. Her husband was the only issue of his deceased parents. But he died of cancer after 5 and half years of marriage leaving Sarala on her own with three little children. After his death, Sarala had to vacate her husband's quarters where they lived. But she had no place to go to in her husband's village. Her widowed mother and younger brother, who came from the village at the time of bereavement, requested her to go back to the native home with them. Accordingly, after performing the sraddha ceremony of her husband, she went away with her mother to stay in her parental family. "But it was a big family with nine children", reported Sarala. "We were seven sisters, including me, of whom three were still unmarried. My two brothers were married but were unable to maintain even their own wives and children. They were cultivating other people's land on *adhi* (share-cropping) system. Though we tried to adjust with the situation, I did not like to be a burden on them. So, being helpless, my younger brother tried to find out a job for me. At last he informed me about a job of polythene bagmaker in an industrial unit in Guwahati and I came to the city with him to take up this job", she concluded.

A widow living in rented house or quarters, allotted in the name of her husband, have to vacate the house after the husband's death. She neither can afford a house nor rent one immediately after husband's death. Such circumstances create problems to many widows in the town following the death of husband.

Nandita was living in a rented house in Guwahati with her husband and two children. Her husband died after eleven years of their married life. After her husband's death it became a problem for her to pay the monthly house rent of Rs. 450.00. Her only brother suggested her to come and stay with him in their father's house. Accordingly, she shifted to her father's house for shelter and security in the same city.

Subhasini's husband was a lower division assistant in the Railway Department. They were staying in the allotted quarters in Guwahati with their five children. After ten years of married life, Subhasini's husband died and she faced much difficulty. She had studied only up to Class IV and therfore it was difficult for her to get a job. She also had to vacate Railway quarters. As she reported, there was no place to stay in her father-in-law's house with her five children, though it was in the same town. Narrating her difficulties after widowhood, she said : "To overcome my difficulties, my father brought me back to his house situated in the city".

From the above cases, it can be surmised that changing patterns of behaviour of husband's kin, combined with new opportunities for education and employment as well as break-down of traditional joint family system pave the way for young widows to move out of the deceased husband's house and face life as single women. In the sample, 52.5 per cent of the widows left their husbands' home after the death of the husband. Those that remained at husbands' home formed 47.5 per cent of the sample. But it is to be noted that 40 per cent actually remained in the (now denuded) nuclear family of the husband, that is to say, even during the husbands' life time, they had formed their own new separate nuclear family consisting of husband, wife, and children only. The widows who stayed in the original joint family of the husband formed a small part (7.5 per cent) of the sample.

After leaving the husbands' home, the widows have to go either to their parents' home or to some working women's hostel or to rented houses or to the home for the destitutes. Where they live thereafter, where they work, and how they adjust themselves to the new situations, is discussed in details in Part Three.

6

SINGLE STATUS THROUGH BROKEN MARRIAGE

The Hindus consider marriage as a sacrament which is indissoluble in life. The duties of husband and wife toward each other have been described by several Hindu writers. According to Manu the wife's marital tie and duty do not come to an end even if the husband were to sell or abandon her. However, examining carefully the earlier Dharmasastra literature, Altekar observes that divorce was permitted before the beginning of the Christian era under certain well-defined circumstances. To support his argument, he says that "... even Manu himself observes elsewhere in his book that a wife is not to blame if she abandons a husband, who is impotent, insane, or suffering from an incurable or contagious disease" (1978:83). But the traditional Hindu women who were expected to be *patibrata* (i.e., devoted to husband) accepted their lots most submissively and devotedly. "It is rather illogical to think that such a traditional Hindu women ever dared to take advantage of the provisions made by the law-givers for obtaining divorce" (Pothen 1987:39). Indian sociologists therefore say that divorce is not known to Hindu institution of marriage (Prabhu 1963:226) which continues to be a sacrament (Kapadia 1988 : 168).

"Though the Hindu marriage was an indissoluble sacrament

till the Hindu Marriages Act of 1954-55, there were provisions even before that for a marriage to be dissolved. The first legislation with regard to the dissolution of marriage was probably enacted by Kolhapur State in the 1920's. The State of Baroda followed suit in 1942. The Bombay Government also passed an Act in 1947 permitting divorce. Madras and Saurashtra followed the example of Bombay in 1949 and 1952 respectively" (Mehta 1975 : 6). Since it has now received a legal validity, the conception of Hindu marriage as a sacrament has undergone many changes. The number of divorce is on the increase in modern society.

As in the other parts of the country, the women of Assam are also learning to stand on their own feet. Because of educational and occupational opportunities, the feeling of dependence on others is gradually disappearing among them. They are not entering into various services. As a result, male dominance is not as pervasive as in the past in the urban Assamese society. A woman who has her independent income is not likely to be very submissive. The men also may not like to give up their dominance so easily. Lack of co-ordination or a genuine understanding between the married partners leads to divorce or separation.

The family may break up either through separation or through formal divorce. The divorced woman is legally free to remarry but a separated woman is not. To study the existing status of a woman and her need to adjust in society, the distinction between divorced and separated status is important.

The percentage of respondents whose marriages were broken without going to any court for legal relief is very high (76.6%). They were classified as 'separated women', living separately from their husbands with or without children. In the present study separation can be taken as an index of instability in conjugal bonds because co-residence of spouses is the norm in the Assamese society.

The percentage of divorced women, who were partly benefited by the legal relief, is very low, being only 23.4. The causes of this low percentage is primarily due to lack of awareness and financial resources to move the court. Another reason is the fear of social insecurity which prevents her from resorting to divorce even with the marriage is very unhappy.

Background factors

Before analysing the various circumstances which pushed

these women to the single status of this category, it is necessary to have an idea of certain background factors. These factors include mainly the socio-cultural context where the respondents had been brought up and the type of their marriage which might have been solemnised with or without negotiation or consent of the two families. These factors play an important part in the decision for separation or divorce. Assessing the influencing factors in a study of divorced or separated Hindu women, Mehta observes, "The problems they faced before and after marriage were closely related to the strata of society they came from and into which they had been married" (1975:3). Moreover, information concerning the socio-economic and cultural backgrounds of the spouses is important is as much as it could be related to their behaviour pertaining to marital dissolution (Pothen 1987:54).

i. *The socio-cultural context* :

The socio-cultural environment (rural, semi-urban and urban) in which individuals grow up exercises different sort of influences on the women concerned. This often creates problems of subsequent adjustment. The women covered in this study are from families living in towns as well as rural areas of Assam. Among them there were fourteen who were born and brought up in urban areas while the rest were of rural origin and upbringing.

The fathers of the fourteen urban single women were either salaried employees or businessmen. Nine were found to be salaried employees and five self-employed businessmen. It has been found that all the fourteen urban single women come from fairly well-do-do families. These women had received higher education up to college level. Educational level of women is an important factor in legal divorce. Before marriage, four obtained M.A. degree, five B.A. and five others had passed High School leaving examination.

Five of these educated women could get teaching jobs giving them independent income even before their marriage.

The sample shows that sixteen women hail from rural areas. Their parents were poor peasants having no land of their own but cultivating as share-croppers and tenants of others. These women had little or no education and no independent earnings. Before marriage, they had simply been assisting their mothers in household work.

ii. *Type of marriage* :

The manner in which a marriage is solemnised affects the life of a divorced or separated woman, since marriage is the foundation of important legal rights and obligations (Desai 1986:705).

Marriage, arranged by the respective families of the bride and bridegroom through family level negotiations, is considered most appropriate both in urban and rural areas of Assam. Of the total women in the sample, 73.3 per cent entered the marriage through negotiation.

But in modern Assamese society, deviation is found. Many girls voice their opinion to marry a boy of their choice. When marriage is mutually settled, the boy and the girl bring the matter to the notice of their respective friends or near kin who then sound the parents about the affair. When the parents do not give their consent the boy and girl get themselves registered as husband and wife under the relevant law. In the present study 23.3 per cent of the respondents were married according to their own choice or without the consent of their parents.

Some women, born and brought up in the traditional rural milieu, could not marry according to their own choice. They also felt shy to disclose their choice and therefore married by way of elopement. The percentage of such marriage is 3.4 in the sample. Elopement can be considered, sometimes, as a preliminary stage of marriage settlement. The parents generally formalise the marriage after elopement.

Whether or not a marriage is solemnised through negotiation between the two families has some impact on the stability of the marriage itself.

Where a marriage is settled by negotiation between the two families, the kin are actively associated at every stage of its solemnisation. The marriage bond is not confined to the spouses only, but binds the kin on both sides. Kinship thus creates a sort of 'umbrella' shielding and protecting the marriage. It is then not very easy for either of the spouses to get separated on flimsy grounds or on counts which are not beyond mending. This cementing factor of kinship is largely absent in the marriage by mutual choice only. The kin members do not feel any responsibility for protecting such a marriage and therefore may take no interest whether it breaks or continues.

This is not to say that divorce or separation does not take place in negotiated marriage. But kin involvement remains one of the most important cementing factors to ensure the stability of a marriage. There are, however, some factors which may go beyond the kin's capacity to mend. Conjugal life is one of the most complex aspects of social life. It is built on the foundation of love and affection; where these are eroded or absent, the conjugal relationship crumbles down gradually. Even in a situation where love and affection between the spouses are present, factors like intrigue by familial kin, and their nagging and interference cause irritation and unhappiness that ultimately lead to divorce or separation. From this point of view, the kin influence may not always be beneficial and it may not always contribute towards the stability of marriage. Interference by relatives may be a potent factor towards destabilisation of marriage.

Causes of divorce or separation

Analysing divorce and separation cases in the sample as well as some cases from judicial court,[12] the cases have been grouped under five broad categories as outlined in Table 20.

Table 20

Causes of dissolution of marriage

Causes	*Divorce* *Number*	*Per cent*
Bigamy	12	25.0
Adultery	10	21.0
Cruelty	15	31.2
Unwed motherhood	3	6.2
Disappearance of husband	4	8.3
Causes not known	4	8.3
	48	100.0

Cruelty as a cause is found in 31.2 per cent of the cases. It is

[12] In addition to the 30 cases collected by direct contact with women, the researcher also studied 18 divorce and separtation cases from court records, in order to make the study broad-based. The total number of cases of divorced and separated women thus comes to 48 in Table 20.

revealed that cruelty does not occur only among the spouses[13], but also between the married woman and her in-laws.

The cause for separation being unwed motherhood is only 6.2. It is a very rare occurrence in the Assamese society for which a marriage may be dissolved.

Some of the women did not like to disclose the causes of their divorce or separation, because, divorce or separation is a personal tragedy as marriage is an intimate exclusive relationship of the couple. The percentage where the causes were not known is 8.3. These cases were taken only to examine the problems of their readjustment in society after attaining single status. It may be noted that generally there is not one solitary cause but a combination of causes that lead to the dissolution of a marriage. But the dominant cause can be easily traced and the classification mentioned above is based on the dominant causes.

i. *Bigamy* :

Monogamy is the general rule in the Assamese Hindu society. It is the most desirable form of marriage. Any other arrangement is generally not anticipated. Bigamous marriage is an exception rather than norm, especially after the enactment of the Hindu Marriage Act 1955. Formerly, before the commencement of the Act, it was practised mainly by a wealthy few to raise their status by having more than one wife or by those who had no issue from the first wife. But in the contemporary Assamese Hindu society, bigamy is one of the major causes for which a marriage may be dissolved. In the collected cases, bigamous marriages were either concealed from the first wife or were effected deliberately by a man with a view to compelling the first wife to separate. In the sample, bigamy is found to constitute the second most important cause of a broken marriage.

Some cases are cited here to indicate the effect of bigamy which pushed the women to their single status.

> Gita, aged 34 at the time of interview, was the only issue of a respectable Kayastha family. She was born and brought up in the city and was a brilliant student. When she was studying engineering, Gita fell in love with a

[13] The expression 'spouse' means a lawfully married husband or wife.

> senior student of the same college and agreed to marry him. The boy's parents who were orthodox Brahmans did not give their consent. But the girl's parents agreed and married her away according to the regular Hindu custom. The couple lived together as husband and wife in a rented house in the city. Meanwhile, Gita's husband obtained his engineering degree and got a job in a reputed firm. But he did not allow Gita to complete her study. He wanted her to be a regular housewife instead of going in for a career. Gita reported, "My husband was not in favour of continuing study and so did not allow me to complete my engineering course. As we had no issue for about seven years of our marriage, I began to feel very lonely at home, specially during the day. In the absence of may husband during his office hours, I, therefore, used to go to my mother's place to pass the time. I had a mind to utilise the day time in study and prepare for some sort of a career. But I could not persuade my husband to agree. He did not like women going in for a job. He wanted me only as a companion to go visiting or to a party or to a movie. But I was not accustomed to such a life". Gita further said, "The real erosion of the marriage started when I used to stay frequently in my mother's house for ever longer period, leaving my husband alone".

A woman's excessive interest in career making may be detrimental to her marital adjustment. If she cannot give time and attention for her domestic responsibilities, the husband feels discontented and neglected.

> After seven years of marriage, Gita gave birth to a child and she became absorbed in rearing up the child. But gradually she noticed that though her husband was nice to her, he was not a sincere companion. He began to avoid her company and used to come back home late in the evenings. Gita felt that she had been unfairly treated by her husband. She frankly admitted that she had heard from her friends that her husband was considered very attractive by other women and one of them was after him. It was also informed that he had started visiting the house of one young widow with whom he had developed intimacy. Gita said that her pride self-esteem was badly hurt and as the tension at home grew day by day, her respect

for her husband weakened. Their relationship deteriorated from bad to worse.

It was alleged that her husband started to ill-treat her and his one year-old son. At last he deserted her and the child and started residing in various hotels in the city. Having been left alone at home, Gita ultimately left for her parental house, along with the child. Her husband never came to her again. He married the aforementioned widow from whom he had a child. This was before the settlement of divorce.

Bakul, 38, was a college lecturer. She was married to an established lawyer by way of negotiation between the two families. She did not give up her job after marriage and the couple were staying in their own house in the city. She had three children by her husband. "But after about five years of our marriage", Bakul said, "the happiness in the family began to ruin. I could notice the change in my husband's behaviour and also know about his extramantal relationship with a non-Assamese woman". She informed that her relationship with her husband was not at all harmonious. Therefore, she asked her husband one day about the affair. The real difficulties, as she reported, between her husband and herself arose from this time on. Bakul also informed that the said lady started to visit their house and join in the quarrels that took place between Bakul and her husband. She even sometimes stayed in a separate bed-room in the house. The situation now became absolutely unbearable for her. Ultimately her husband filed a divorce case against her and married that lady. Therefore he moved into a separate house leaving Bakul and his little children behind.

In the two cases mentioned above, erosion of the married life started before the actual bigamous marriage.

Padma, 39, is a high-ranking government officer. She was married to a professional person of the city by negotiation between the two families. The marriage was celebrated according to the Hindu rites and customs. Unfortunately, they could not pull on together and soon after marriage Padma left her husband's house.

> According to Padma her husband is a person having no sense of morality. Before marriage he had affairs with a girl whose house in another town he visited often. The affair continued even after the marriage. Seeing the cold attitude of her husband after marriage Padma could gather the real reasons. Her husband also started mixing with other girls in Guwahati. "He was often found with them in manner not expected from a man of his status", Padma said. The husband filed a divorced case and obtained a decree and married another lady by registration. The separation between Padma and her husband was thus complete.

All the three bigamy cases, described above, occurred in the city life of the women. But instance of bigamy as a cause of dissolution of marriage is also found among the women of rural areas. These cases can be considered as separation, as they did not come to the court for a decree of divorce.

> Damayanti belonged to a traditional family from a rural area of the lower Assam. She was married to a driver of the same place, working under the Assam Electricity Board. Her husband was posted in Shillong and took Damayanti there. During the time of delivery of her first child, he took her home and kept her under the care of his mother and other members of his family. Strangely, however, even after a long period had elapsed he did not return to take her and the child back in Shillong. One day she was informed by a villager that her husband had meanwhile married a girl of Garo community in Shillong. She was shocked and discussed the matter with all the members of her husband's family to find out a way for her own livelihood. There was no formal separation between Damayanti and her husband but they never saw each other again.
>
> Damayanti's husband being posted out of his own place was not under the observation of his kingroup. Her absence also gave him the chance to have contact with another woman in Shillong. He was able to lead a life in which there was little fear of reprimand from his kingroup.
>
> Tamilini came from a Brahmin family of a village at Nalbari district. Her father was a government officer and

got her educated in the village school. She passed her matriculation in 1972 and was given in marriage to a boy of the same district selected by her father. The boy was an office assistant in a government office. He was the only son of his parents and was therefore very obedient and dependent on them. As she reported, her husband's mother thought Tamalini was not a good match for her son and found fault in everything that she did. Her husband's two unmarried sisters joined their mother in ill-treating her. She said, "After my first delivery I had to pass my days with great difficulties. Without proper nourishment I had to work hard in doing all the household work along with taking care of my new-born baby. I also did not get any sympathy or affection from my husband. Soon I conceived again. So it became a problem for me to take care of the little child along with other household work. I could not satisfy my dominant mother-in-law in my physical condition. I had no alternative except coming to my parents' house for my proper care. My husband also agreed to that and accompanied me to my parents' house. But after that he did not come to me. I was informed by a man of my husband's village that he had married another girl of his mother's choice. It was informed after six days of his remarriage. Surprised, I went to my husband's place with my father and the child to confirm the matter. I saw the new wife living there".

She further reported, "My father tried to convince my husband that I had a right to stay there as a legal wife. My father also tried to assert that it is the duty of my husband to take care of me in my pregnant condition. After this, my father left leaving me and my child behind." As she reported, Tamalini started her life with the co-wife and tried to adjust herself to the new situation. After about sixteen days of her arrival in husband's place, she gave birth to a male child. She informed, "But after delivery, I was treated like an animal, as I could not perform any household work due to my impurity for a month. Nobody helped me during that period. For another three months I tried to adjust to the situation, but I could not. Being helpless, with two children and without any proper maintenance from my husband, I left my husband's place for ever and took shelter in my parents' house".

In the rural areas of Assam, the bigamy is sometimes practised due to childlessness of the first wife. A barren daughter-in-law is very much neglected in her husband's house and even considered as inauspicious.

Kanika's case is worth citing. Her husband was a carpenter from a nearby village of Kamrup district. She did not conceive till two years after her marriage. For that reason, her mother-in-law began to ill-treat her. Kanika reported, "My husband also did not want to talk to me and did not behave with me properly. Being helpless, I informed the matter to my brother. One day my brother and uncle came to me and they talked to my husband. With his permission, my brother took me away to his place for a few days for a change. But during this period, I came to know that my husband had married again. I was deeply shocked after getting that news and never returned to my husband's house.

Another woman, Aikon, was from a village of Nalbari district. She was the only daughter of her parents and so she was very much loved by them. Her father was a poor agriculturist and so he wanted to marry his daughter away immediately after she attained puberty. He therefore arranged her marriage with Bhabendra who ran a vegetable vending shop in the market in Guwahati. But Aikon, who was then only 14 years of age, had no consent in this marriage. This, because she knew that Bhabendra had another wife. As the first wife had no issue, Bhabendra wanted to marry Aikon with the hope of getting a child. However, Aikon was compelled to obey her poor father and the marriage was celebrated. It was thought by her parents that Aikon could live happily with her husband in Guwahati as he had a good income from his business. But after the marriage, Bhabendra did not take Aikon to stay in Guwahati and she had to stay in her husband's village with the co-wife and mother-in-law. Aikon narrated, "For the first few days, it was well and good. But after about a month it became difficult for me to tolerate the attitude and ill-treatment of the co-wife. My husband used to visit home once in a week. I told him everything, but he could not give any solution. I therefore came to my parents' house to stay there for some time. I was accompanied by my husband and he assured me that he would take me back after arranging a separate establishment for me in Guwahati. But when he did nothing of sort, after I had stayed for four months in my parents' house, I went to my husband's house with my mother hoping for a better adjustment in the family. My mother-in-law was ill-disposed towards me and she also began to behave with me very badly. Being helpless in the absence of my husband, one day I convened a meeting (*mel*) of the village elders in which I said that it was impossible for me to stay in such a condition where nobody was there to look after me. The matter was discussed in the meeting and the villagers gave me assurance that my husband would make a separate arrangement for me to live with him. I therefore came again to my parents' house to stay there till the assured arrangement. The matter was informed to my husband through a villager and he also agreed. That day I came out along from my mother-in-law's place leaving all my utensils and furniture. I did not bring anything except a few clothes for daily use. My husband came to see me four times in my parents' home. But eventually he ceased to come and stopped giving the money for the maintenance". Aikon had no other alternative then to remain in her parents' house. Ultimately separation took place between Aikon and her husband.

In all these cases, it is seen that bigamy itself was the result of different causes, like childlessness, domineering attitude of mother and sisters of husbands, incompatibility of attitudes, affairs with other women to which the husbands succumbed, and so on. But whatever might be the cause of bigamy it ended in each case by way of dissolution of the original marriage and the wife became a single woman, filled with bitterness and frustration.

ii. *Adultery* :

The third largest group (21 per cent) of broken marriages in the sample was due to adultery. In the Hindu Marriage Act 1955, adultery is defined as consensual sexual intercourse between a married person and another person of the opposite sex during the subsistence of the marriage (Desai 1986:776). If even only one of the parties to the act is married, it may constitute adultery for the purposes of dissolution of that marriage.

The cases cited below for illustrating adultery may look like almost bigamy cases cited before, since a married man was having affairs with an unmarried woman. The cases are, no doubt, similar but not the same. In the cases cited earlier, the affairs ultimately ended in the second marriage of the man which thus constituted bigamy and the first marriage was broken as a consequence of bigamous marriage. Bigamy was thus the final cause for dissolution of marriage narrated earlier. In the case cited below, the original marriage broke down before the extra-marital relationship of a spouse became a bigamous in nature. The cases have been studied in respect of both the husband and wife.

> Rumi was studying for Master's degree at the time of her marriage. The marriage was negotiated by the families of the bride and the groom. The bridegroom was the only son of his widowed mother and was a company executive staying in the same city.
>
> The marriage was celebrated according to traditional Hindu rites and customs. Rumi started her married life by trying her best to adjust herself with the members of the family of her husband. For about a month she was happy with the family. But gradually as she reported, she noticed an indifference and coldness in the attitude of her husband. He used to come home very late and spent very little time with her. He tried to convince her that he was too busy with his office work and therefore he had no time at all to be with her. Gradually Rumi became unhappy with the behaviour of her husband. She was shocked when her husband began to give some of her personal properties, gifted in her marriage, to his mother and unmarried sister. He gave her new double bed to his mother and the sewing maching to his sister for her personal use, without Rumi's consent. Rumi reported, "My sentiment was touched when I had to give unwillingly my expensive foam mattress to my mother-in-law to satisfy my husband". She further stated, "This was the point from where our conjugal life became unhappy. I tried to tolerate his caustic remarks keeping myself silent. But I could not tolerate the matter

when I came to know that he was having an extra-marital relationship with another woman even from before the marriage. All the neighbours knew of the affair and informed me about it. The man married me just to satisfy his mother. He did not stop his old relationship with the said woman. After knowing the facts, I informed the matter to my parents".

Rumi further narrated her case, "One day I asked my husband about the matter and I was severely beaten up for that. My mother-in-law and sister-in-law did not try to interfere. So life became miserable for me. I therefore decided to leave my husband's place as soon as possible. Some time later, one morning I was compelled to leave his house. After my morning bath when I was praying in the *gosai-ghar*, my husband entered and threw away the earthen lamp, incense and other sacred articles. He then dragged me out from the *gosai-ghar* and began to beat me up and remarked 'Prayer is not necessay for a woman like you'. I was shocked by his outburst. I did not know what to do. I retired to the bed-room where too hot exchange of words took place. At that moment I decided to leave the house. When my husband left for office, I took the chance and quietly came out from the house without informing my decision to anybody. Only with few clothes and articles in my bag, I left the house alone. From that day I never visited my husband's house".

Rumi is an educated town-bred woman who studied up to M.A. level. Instances of illterate rural women have also been found whose marriages were dissolved because of adultery.

Bhanu, 22 at the time of interview, is the daughter of a Brahmin priest (*purohit*) of a village in Kamrup district. She was married away at the tender age of nine. She could adjust herself in the new family as one of the members, taking all the responsibilities of a daughter-in-law. As she informed, she could establish good relationship with the family members of her husband. Bhanu reported, "But unfortunately, from some of my neighbours and relatives, I came to know after about three months of our marriage that my husband had an illicit relationship with a girl from a neighbouring village. So I tried to confirm the fact. One day, I asked my husband about the affair but he tried to evade me and there was an altercation that night. As a result, our marital relationship began to deteriorate gradually". Later on, it was found that her husband was planning to marry that girl very soon. After knowing the fact, Bhanu had a frank discussion with her mother-in-law and then left the husband's home for her parental house and never went back. "But I did not inform anything to my unfaithful husband", Bhanu added.

So was the case of Dipali. She was from a village of Sibsagar district and got married at the early age of fifteen. She had two children by her husband. But he was very irregular in staying at home. He often spent his nights elsewhere. On enquiry she came to know that he had relationships with many women and was a man of bad character. He neglected the maintenance of the family along with his two little children. "But I tried to adjust myuself with him only for the welfare of my children". Depali narrated, "Things came to such a pass that ultimately I had to leave my husband's house. Having no alternative I came out to my brother's house instead of my father's house. I did not like to go to my father's house because of my stepmother".

In another case, an educated and well-employed woman stated that illicit relationship of her husband with his elder brother's wife was the reason for the breaking up of marriage. Her husband was an engineer. After marriage they lived in a rented house in Guwahati. She stated that while residing there in the rented house, her husband started to behave with her in a harsh manner and gradually he began to torture her both physically and mentally. One day, her husband went away with his belongings without saying anything to her. She therefore went to her parents' house, informed the matter to her parents and she herself, accompanied by her father and other relatives, made enquiries of her husband in different places. Later on, she came to learn that her husband, after leaving the rented house, went to his elder brother's house who too lived in the city. She requested him to come back to the rented house to live with her, but he refused. Having no other alternative, she vacated the rented house and shifted to her parents' house. The husband then filed a petition for legal separation.

In the following cases, it is the woman who committed adultery which ultimately led to dissolution of the marriage.

Sobha was born and brought up in Guwahati and studied in a reputed college in a big city outside Assam. Her's was an arranged marriage with a well-placed engineer from a respectable family. Many young engineers were working under him and they used to come to their house. One of them became very friendly and intimate with Sobha. They began to enjoy their club life together in the evening. Things came to such a pass that the husband accused her of infidelity. Subsequently, separation took place and she left her husband's house to stay with her parents in Guwahati along with her two grown up daughters. She took away the car, once gifted to her by her husband.

Niru hails from a traditional Brahmin family of Upper Assam. She was married in 1945 at the age of thirteen before attaining puberty. Following the customary practice, she could not reside in her husband's house before attainment of puberty and performances of *santi-biyu*[14] with the husband. So Niru stayed in her parents' house. During that time, Niru was given a chance by her parents to take a course in music at home and a music teacher was appointed for her. Gradually the teacher became very close to her and they soon fell in love. Meanwhile, Niru attained puberty and was growing into a lovely girl. Eventually Niru gave birth to a child at her parents' house before performing the *Santi-biya* with her husband. On hearing this, the husband refused to take her and the illegitimate child. As a result, separation took place between Niru and her husband and she could not go to stay with him.

In another case, a couple married in 1961 according to Hindu rites, had a child born to them in 1962. There was,

---

[14] Santi-biya : Purifying marriage after a girl's first menstruation in Brahmin families, before joining her husband, in traditional Assamese Society.

however, no further issue. They led a happy married life. But since 1967 the wife showed signs of indifference. Ultimately her husband discovered that she had developed an illicit relationship with another man who used to visit her frequently during his absence. One day, by design, the husband came home at an unexpected hour and saw the man and his wife in a compromising situation. He then submitted a petition for legal divorce.

In the following case the husband was a senior executive of a reputed company. But after about a month or so of marriage, the husband came to know that his wife used to go out by herself practically every day after he left for office and she would come just before he got back for lunch. These were told by his servant but she had not mentioned at all about those outings to him at any time. Once when he returned from office he did not find his wife. She came back at about 6 P.M. and on being asked, she curtly replied that she had gone for a drive towards the airport with one of his friends. After that she did not talk for the rest of the evening. Another time the same thing happened again when the husband reached home. On being asked about her absence, she said that it was none of his business to ask such questions. The husband explained to her that he certainly did not mind her going out, but she should leave word where she was going and at what time she would be back home, to which she did not reply at all.

There were a number of occasions when the wife gave vent to her anger violently. On one occasion, a heavy time piece was thrown at him which struck him on the head. On another occasion, she screamed and took off her wedding ring and jewellery and threw them all over the room shouting at the top of her voice, "your mother gave them to me, take them away. I do not want them". A few incidents which came to the knowledge of the husband left him in no doubt that his wife was having an extra-marital affair with one of his friends during his absence. The husband came to know about two incidents of adultery when he was in Calcutta for some office work. The husband requested her not to meet that person, but she continued to meet him in his absence.

> Therefore, ultimately on the ground of cruelty to the husband and the adultery committed by his wife, the husband filed the suit for a decree of divorce.

Thus it may be concluded that extra-marital relation of either spouse is a major cause for marital disruption.

iii. *Cruelty* :

In the sample, cruelty has been found to be the cause of the largest number (31.2 per cent) of broken marriages. The legal conception of cruelty and the kind of the degree of it necessary to constitute a matrimonial offence has not been defined in any Indian statute on marriage or divorce. The accepted legal meaning in England as also in India of this expression has been "conduct of such a character as to have caused danger to life, limb or health (bodily or mental), or as to give rise to a reasonable apprehension of such danger" (Desai 1986:781).

In the present study, drunkenness, physical torture, abusive language, envious behaviour, or ill-treatment by the husband or the mother-in-law or the sisters-in-law have been found to be the various forms of cruelty perpetrated on the women. According to Desai "Drunkenness, *per se*, is not cruelty. But persistent drunkenness after warnings that such a course of conduct is inflicting pain on the other spouse and if the offending spouse knows that it is injuring the health of that spouse, may well amount to cruelty. Such drunkenness, if it is combined with other acts of ill-treatment, as it usually is, may obviously be a factor of great importance" (1986 : 791).

> Manimala, a Master's degree holder, was a school teacher and married to a businessman. Both of them were permanent residents of Guwahati. She had a child by him. But as stated by Manimala, from the first night to her stay with him she felt abhorred by his excessively drinking. She could not bear even the smell of alcohol. Manimala urged him again and again to reduce his drinking in the interest of their conjugal happiness. But he did not care for her mental condition and sought only carnal enjoyment. On the other hand, she felt a great revulsion and could not be responsive. Manimala reported, "Because of my negative attitude to enjoy sex with such a man, I had been physically tortured by him. You can see the scars on my body".

Narrating his cruelty she further added that he spent all his income on drinks and she had to run the house with her small income from teaching. Unable to carry on any longer, she with her baby-in-arms came to her parental house.

Same was the case of Pratima. She was a graduate and was married to an engineer. Both of them were permanent residents of the city. As she reported, Pratima's husband was a heavy drinker. She could not bear his drinking, specially at night. When she trid to request him to avoid liquor, she was always beaten up by her husband. For the first few days she tried to adjust herself with the situation. As time passed, the cruelty became worse and intolerable. Being helpless, she informed the matter to her parents. One day her mother came to visit her. Her husband was in office at that time. By taking the chance of his absence, Pratima left with her mother, handing over the key of the house to the next door neighbour. She did not go back again to her husband's house.

Bina was married to one Tarani according to Hindu rites performed at the temple of Kamakhya. He was a Railway pointsman and they lived in Guwahati with their three children.

One day a girl named Manibala came to their house. From Manibala, Bina learnt that Tarani had another wife by a previous marriage at a village of Nagaon district. Manibala was the daughter of Tarani by that wife. These things were not disclosed to Bina earlier. After Manibala's visit, Tarani began to ill-treat Bina and even beat her up. Once he attacked her with a dao. He persisted in beating her every now and then. Her life became miserable and at last it was impossible for her to live with him any longer. She had to take shelter in the house of Tarani's sister's husband with her children in another area of the city. Then she filed an application for divorce in the court.

Quarrelsome nature of woman is also a form of cruelty. Often it is not the husband but the wife who behaves cruelly towards the husband.

Karabi and her husband were both lower division

assistants in two different offices in Guwahati. They lived in a rented house. But soon after marriage, Karabi's behaviour towards her husband became peculiar and often violent. She approached him, taunted him and always complained to him about this thing or that. Sometimes she rushed towards him with the gesture of assault. Ultimately, after about six months of their marriage, the woman deserted her husband and since then she has been living in the residence of her father in Guwahati without having any connection with her husband. He then filed a petition for a decree of divorce.

iv. *Unwed motherhood* :

Unwed motherhood may be also one of the causes of divorce or separation. Pregnancy through some one other than the spouse before marriage is a recognised ground for divorce in the court of law. But such cases are not very common in Assam. In the sample, the percentage of such cases was found to be only 6.2.

Two such cases are mentioned below :

Following the custom prevalent in the Assamese society, Durga as bride came to her husband's house on the following day of the marriage. Both of them were from a district of lower Assam. On the first night of their conjugal life, the husband could understand for the first time that the bride was already pregnant before marriage and immediately he left her alone and lived completely separated from her in the first night and on the following morning he came to Guwahat where he is working in a government office. Living a few days in the husband's house with his old mother, the bride went to her father's house stating that she would undergo some treatment for her illness during the absence of the husband. After some days, Durga again returned to the husband's house and when the husband went home in vacation, he asked her to leave the house. She then confessed before him and gave him in writing that she was pregnant by some other man before marriage. The husband did never live together with the wife that night. On the following day when Durga complained severe abdominal pain, the husband informed her father whose house is about eight miles away from his house, to come immediately to take the charge of his wife.

Durga's two elder brothers came and took her to Guwahati and admitted her in the Gauhati Medical College Hospital. Next morning she gave birth to a male child and a few days after being discharged from the hospital she had been taken to her brothers' house. A case was then filed by the husband and divorce was granted.

In the next case also the facts were similar. On the following day of Jasoda's marriage, the suspicion began to work in the mind of her husband. Ultimately, Josada had to confess that she was running about seven months pregnancy with one who is her sister's husband.

As the husband was ignorant about the pregnancy of his bride, and as the marital intercourse of the husband did not take place since the discovery of the bride's pregnancy by some other person, he prayed to dissolve the marriage by a decree of nullity.

v. *Disappearance of husband* :

Disappearance of the husbands is another significant cause for separation, though the reasons for it is not always known. Disappearance results in grave problems, especially, if the woman is not living in joint family.

Hemanti got married to a man who held an office assistant's job in the Railway Department at Siliguri. She was working in a Lower primary school. She was staying in a rented house in Guwahati. After marriage both of them were thus staying separately in two different places. Hemanti was told by her husband that after getting a quarters he would take her to Siliguri to stay with him. Meanwhile, he used to come to her place to stay together for two or three days. They continued their conjugal life in this fashion. But as the time of her first delivery he could not come to attend her due to some heavy office work. After about eight months of the birth of the child, one day he came to see the child and the very next morning he returned to his place of work. As stated by Hemanti, "That was the last visit of my husband. Since then I do not know anything about him. I wrote to him many letters, but did not receive any answer. I am not keeping any correspondence with him as I do not know his whereabouts at present". Disappearance created much hardship to her. It was extremely inconvenient and problematic to Hemanti to manage her household duties as well as her working life with her little child.

Ilora also could not inform about her husband's whereabouts. When enquired she informed that after marriage they were living jointly with the brothers of her husband. It was a happy family. After about three years of their marriage, her husband went away leaving her alone with the little child, without informing anybody. She reported "I have already spent 28 years in the same joint family of my husband with a hope of his return". As she was living in a joint family, Illora did not face much problems like Hemanti.

In another case, Apati was the only daughter of her parents. She got married at the age of 14. Her husband was from a village of Kamrup district. He was working as a peon. The family was a happy one. They had three children. "After six years of our married life", Apati stated, "one day, my husband told me that he would visit Guwahati as he had some work there. But he did not return home from the trip. He also did not inform anything to anybody. So, we, the members of the family became anxious and began to search for him. My husband's younger brother and some of our relatives tried to find out the whereabouts of my husband". Apati still uses vermillion on her forehead and harbours the hope that her husband would return one day.

Duration of married life

The duration of married life of the 30 women in the sample has been analysed to determine the length of married life at the time of dissolution of marriage. The maximum duration of married life is thirteen years and the minimum only one month. The situation is shown in Table 21.

It is seen that shorter the duration of married life, higher the number of respondents. This is because problems of adjustments with a new man or a new family arise generally at the beginning of married life. Gradually, after passing the years, —love, affection and regard of a married couple become ever deeper and chances of dissolution lessen. The maturity of married life helps in cementing marital relation. But when a marriage dissolves at an early age, the woman finds comparatively less difficulty in readjustments. As a scholar observes "They still have chances of finding a partner of their choice, their enthusiasm and energy to live is yet unfinished, their habits and interests are yet pliable and they exhibit a greater degree of adaptability. Though several other factors influence the post-divorce adjustment, age is a very important one "(Pothen 1987:183).

Table 21

Duration of married life of the divorcees in the sample

Duration of married life	*Number of divorcees*
Below 2 years	13
2-5 years	6
5-15 years	7
Period not known	4
	30

Age at divorce or separation

Regarding the age at divorce or separation it is found that minimum age was 14 years, while the maximum age was 35 years.

Table 22

Age group of the divorcees at the time of dissolution of marriage

Age group	*Number of divorcees*
15 & below	4
16-20	5
21-25	9
26-30	4
31-35	4
Age not known	4
	30

Table 22 shows that the highest number of women belongs to the age group of 21-25. The number is smaller among the women of higher age group. It can be assumed from the higher number of the respondents in the lower age group that causes of divorce or separation among them may arise due to immaturity of the respondents. In their early age, they are not able to find out a solution amicably to adjust with the husband or with the members of the husband's family.

7

THE UNMARRIED AS SINGLE WOMEN

Since ancient times marriage has been regarded by the Hindus not only as a necessity, but also as a social and religious duty. The Vedic literature describes an unmarried person as unholy. Pointing out a Vedic passage, Altekar (1978:31) notes: "From the religious point of view he remains incomplete and is not fully eligible to participate in sacraments". Therefore oblations offered by a maiden or a bachelor are unacceptable by gods and ancestors. It is mentioned in the epic *Mahabarata* that women ought never to remain unmarried. The *Mahabharata* also tells us that the mortal remains of a maiden can be consigned to flames only after the symbolic performance of marriage after death (*ibid.* 33). The nuptial caremony is considered to be a Vedic sacrament for women. "It is hence that a girl who dies unmarried when she has reached puberty should be united in a sort of marriage with a male of the same caste before she is cremated" (Kapadia 1988:141). Marriage as a form of *samskara* (purification), therefore, occupies an important place in a woman's life. Referring to unmarried girls in Vedic literature, Altekar states that some women began to enter monastic life instead of entering into matrimony to achieve spiritual salvation. But some maidens could not achieve their spiritual salvation. As a result, they had to face public criticism of their position. Many factors induced the society to prevent such abuses by making marriage obligatory for girls. Marriage thus came to be regarded as obligatory for girls by about 300 B.C. (Altekar 1978:32). The evidences from history and Assamese literature show that in Assam also marriage has been made obligatory for girls since very early times. It is learnt that in the Assamese society, marriage of the girls was considered necessary to purify their body (Barua 1972: 200).

The traditional views hold sway among the people of Assam even now. According to this view, girls should not remain unmarried not at least as a matter of choice. To remain unmarried is regarded as exceptional, justified, in exceptional circumstances only.

But in the recent decades, especially since the time of independence, women's participation and achievements in out-of-home activities have slowly changed the traditional conceptions on the role and status of women in the contemporary Assamese society. Because of the changed socialization pattern, opportunities for education and employment of women have come about. The emergence of new socio-conomic conditions have drastically altered women's attitude towards their status and role in society. These changes have encouraged them to make new choices not provided for in the traditional model of society.

The rising rate of literacy in the contemporary Assamese society has increased the age at marriage for women. According to 1971 census, the percentage of married women in Assam has declined where the educational qualification has risen to matriculation and graduation levels (see Table 7, p. 73). Spread of education has brought new ideals among all sections of people, including the women. New socio-economic conditions have opened up new avenues of employment even for women. The shackles of superstition are on the wane among the educated girls and they show a clear trend of making their own choices about their future life. The unmarried status of women is no longer considered to be as exceptional a phenomenon among the urbanised segment of Assamese people as it used to be in the past.

Causes of remaining unmarried

The reasons for which the Assamese women may decide not to marry have been analysed from the collected cases in the sample.

The analysis of cases reveals two main reasons for remaining unmarried :

1. Unmarried status by choice and decision of a woman herself.
2. Unmarried status due to compelling circumstances beyond the control of a woman.

Table 23 shows the number and proportion of women in the sample remaining unmarried because of various causes and factors. The actual circumstances of remaining unmarried will be evident from the following case materials.

Table 23

Causes for remaining unmarried

Causes	*Total*	
	Number	*Per cent*
1. Unmarried status by choice and decision of a woman herself :		
i. Dedication of life to a noble cause	3	7.5
ii. Pursuit of career	4	10.0
iii. Betrayed love or disappointment in love	5	12.5
iv. Parental objection to marry someone of her own choice	5	12.5
2. Unmarried status due to compelling circumstances :		
i. To support to poor parents and siblings	6	15.0
ii. Chronic ailments and physical disabilities	9	22.5
iii. Loss of parents in childhood	3	7.5
iv. Unwed motherhood	5	12.5
	40	100.0

1. Unmarried status by choice and decision of a woman herself

It is found that 42.5 per cent of the respondents, in the sample of unmarried single women, did not enter into matrimony by their own choice or decision. Marriage was avoided by these women for the reasons mentioned below :

i. *Dedication of life to a noble cause* :

As for dedication of life to a noble cause, we may cite the case of Ahalya.

> Ahalya obtained a Master's degree in science from Calcutta University. She, however, was determined from her schooldays to dedicate her life to the freedom struggle. She came into contact with Mahatma Gandhi at the tender age of ten, when Gandhiji visited Assam in 1921, duing the non-cooperation movement. After she passed out of University, she met Gandhiji frequently and decided to remain a celibate with a view to devoting her time and efforts to the cause of the freedom movement and social welfare-oriental activities. She devoted herself particularly to the constructive programmes of Gandhiji for the upliftment of the women of Assam.

> The same was the case with Amiya. She was very religious-minded from her childhood. As she grew up, she was attracted by the teachings of Mahatma Gandhi and jumped into the movement for freedom of the country. Amiya decided to lead the life of a spinster so as to be able to devote all her time and energy to the freedom struggle. She thus remained unmarried for the noble cause of fighting for country's freedom and for the upliftment of womenfolk. She joined the Kasturba Gandhi National Memorial Trust in 1946 to dedicate her life to social work. She said that social work with a spiritual outlook of mind is more peaceful than a life in marriage.

Religion also has an impact on life which induces some women to carry a devoted life without entering into matrimony.

> Bani, 49, said, "A religious life gives much more happiness than a married one". She said that she had a religious bent of mind since her childhood. She listened avidly to the stories of the *Ramayana* and the *Mahabharata* from her parents. She took avid interest in religious discourses. She became a school teacher and led the life of a spinster devoting her leisure time to religious activities.

ii. *Pursuit of career* :

A woman who is ambitious about her career might not wish to enter into matrimony. This kind of life is very rarely found among the Assamese women. "Careers imply a long, if not a lifetime, commitment to moving upward through a series of related occupations and statuses according to a schedule" (International Encyclopaedia of Soc. Sc. 1972 : 252). Women who go after career in this fashion feel that marriage is incompatible with careerism. Married life involves so many duties and obligations towards husband, children and affinal kin that these might hinder the free pursuit of career activities and might actually force married women to alter their career plan. A woman pursuing an ambitious career tends to feel that she cannot submit to this state of affairs and prefers rather to remain unmarried than shoulder the burdens of a married life.

> Arati, 52, is a case in point. She had deliberately opted for the life of a career woman at a very tender age. Being the daughter of a freedom fighter, she had to face economic hardships during the period of freedom struggle. As a consequence, "I had to decide to make my life independent through the pursuit of a suitable career", she said. She gave up the idea of marriage for good and devoted herself to studies for appearing in competitive examinations for government service. She actually did so and succeeded in getting into the Assam Civil Service.

> Sashiprava, 58, devoted her life to an educational career. She made it her sole object in life. She said : "It gives me great pleasure and satisfaction that I am devoting my life to education". According to her, education is necessary for a fuller and happier life. After completing higher education, she ultimately became a teacter in a reputed college. She is also an active member of various social and cultural organizations.

iii. *Betrayed love or disappointment in love* :

Disappointment in love due to betrayal by lover is another factor in pushing a woman into the status of unmarried women. Many women choose to remain unmarried, once they are betrayed by their lovers. They are often unable to recover from deep shock. A sort of cynicism grips them and they begin to lose faith in men and marriage.

Binaya, Kalita by caste, was engaged to one of her college friends belonging to her own caste. She was then studying at the under-graduate level in a reputed college. At that time (1940s) there were very few girl students in the college and parents did not like to send their daughters to co-educational institution. She fall in love with a boy from the same college and came to an agreement to marry him just after he was able to secure a job. The boy, however, betrayed her and married a girl junior to Binaya in the same college. Betrayed by one, whom she genuinely loved, Binaya gave up the idea of marriage itself. She turned down every proposal that came to her family. Her father also did not insist on her marriage against her will and decision. Instead, she was sent to Calcutta by her father to study B.A. She passed out and became a teacher and never married.

Pranati fell in love with a boy while she was studying in Class X. The boy reciprocated the love and promised to marry her. Both of them were from the scheduled caste community and there was no bar to marry each other. The boy visited her parents' house quite often and also the house of her father's brother which was nearby. Unfortunately, her father's brother's daughter also fell in love with the same boy and the parents of this girl immediately arranged their marriage. Pranati was shocked when she came to learnt about it. But she could not protest as the bride was her cousin. She refused all the marriage proposals that came afterwards and determined not to marry in life. Her father tried several times to get her married but she remained adamant. Ultimately, she became a school teacher leading the life of a single woman.

In these cases the suitors were of the same caste as the girls who were born and brought up in the city. In rural areas also similar case has been found.

Padmini had prolonged love-affair with a boy since her school days. They were from a village of lower Assam belonging to same Kayastha case. The two gave words to each other that after the boy had settled down, they would get married. The boy went outside Assam to complete his studies, and changed his mind in the process. After completion of his studies, he married another girl from the same village. Padmini was deeply shocked and felt cheated. She said that from that moment she felt a hatred towards men in general and resolved not to marry in life. In order to lead an independent single life, she studied Law, took the LL.B. degree and started practice as a lawyer.

iv. *Parental objection to marry someone of her own choice :*

As mentioned earlier, marriage in the Assamese society is generally arranged by the way of negotiation between the families of the future bride and the groom. Girls are not usually free to marry according to their own choice. But a new trend has appeared among the educated women especially in the urban areas, to choose their own life partners with or without the consent to the parents. When the parents object, some girls, nevertheless, marry—breaking the ties with their respective parental families. But there are girls who would not go to that extent. They bow down to the parents' objection. At the same time, however, most of them do not agree to marry another person chosen by the parents. They rather choose to remain celibate and devote themselves to some independent pursuits.

> Ila, an engineer, wanted to marry an engineer friend whom she had met in the college. While she was a Hindu the boy was a Muslim. But during their college life they did not think much about the barrier of religion. So they agreed to marry just after completion of their engineering studies. After graduation, the boy was the first to get a job and Ila, without waiting further, disclosed the matter to her parents. The parents had great affection for her, but they just would not give their consent to an interreligious marriage. Ila also did not like to go against the wishes of her loving parents. She said, "I could not hurt my parents' sentiments just to fulfil my own wishes. I did not like to hurt their feelings. That would have been too selfish. But at the same time I could not give my consent to any other marriage proposals". She gave up the idea of marrying at all and decided to remain single.

Sometimes a girl takes such a decision not because of the objection of her own parents but because of the objection of the boy's parents. In either case, she remains a single woman.

> Manika, a Kaibartta by caste, was in love with a boy of Kayastha caste. They agreed to marry; but the parents of the boy would not allow him to marry a girl from another caste which to them was very much lower than theirs in the caste hierarchy. The boy submitted to his parents' objection. Manika was shocked and decided not to enter into matrimony at all.

It is found that parents also obstruct marriage on the ground of the status of the groom.

> Anju, a Master's degree-holder in science, was a gazetted officer. She wanted to marry a boy who, however, was only a graduate. He had an autorickshaw and also owned a shop for electrical goods. The economic condition of the boy's family was also not equal to that of Anju's family. Her parents, therefore, did not favour the proposal. She could not press her parents too much, but decided not the marry any other person and remained single.

The cases reveal that it is often difficult for the parents as well as for the girl to find out a suitable groom of equal or higher status. It is also difficult to find a suitable match for a girl having high education and good job or economic status.

> The case of Sikha is a good example. She had deliberately opted to remain single. She was born and brought up in a family much involved in the sphere of dance and music. Ever since her childhood, she was given help, encouragement and training in dance and music by her family. She excelled in the sphere of performing arts and gave dance recitals in Assam and even outside the State. She earned good amount from her performances. The problem arose in finding a suitable groom who would allow her to continue with her dance recitals even after marriage. It was difficult for her and her parents to find such a person easily. "To keep a balance between my way of life with that of the life of a house-wife would really be a problem for me", Sikha said. So she decided to remain unmarried rather than give up her cultural activities.

Unable to find a life partner of equal status, many women choose to remain single rather than enter into matrimony. They feel that marriage may hinder their pursuit of academic or professional skill, or free pursuit of higher thinking and living.

2. Unmarried status due to compelling circumstances beyond the control of a woman

In the foregoing cases, the women have by and large voluntarily opted for remaining unmarried, though they might, if they so desired, have entered into a life of matrimony. But there are cases where the women have no laternative than to forego marriage. The circumstances have already been mentioned. As much as 57.8 per cent of women in the unmarried single category reflect such circumstances. Few such cases are cited below.

i. Remaining unmarried to give support to poor parents and siblings :

In the patriarchal Assamese society, a woman is at times required to take the responsibilitis of her natal family as a breadwinner. Such circumstances compel her to remain unmarried.

> Uma, aged 48 years, is a superintendent in a government office. She had to start her working life at the age of twenty. The income of her father was not sufficient to maintain the family of four children—of which three were daughters and the fourth a son. Uma was the eldest among the children and she therefore felt much about the future of her only brother and the two younger sisters. Referring to the problems of her family, Uma said, "I had a mind tc complete my college education. But for the sake of the family, I had to take up a job just after appearing in the intermediate examination in 1955. I joined as a lower division assistant and with my small income, I had to think for the educationof my brother, so that he can help the family when he grows up". She narrated the many difficulties and problems she faced in supporting her family and said : "We had to leave our father's ancestral house after the partition of the joint property. We then came to live in a rented house and this caused great hardship. But after I had got the job in a government office, I tried for an official quarters. Fortunately, I got an allotment in my name for a quarters and left the rented house. For several years since then, I was kept busy having to support my parents and siblings. I could not think even of my own future, I had to refuse all marriage proposals for the welfare of my family

members. When my brother obtained a B.A. degree and got a job, it was great relief for me. But by then it was too late for me to think of marriage".

Nayana, a practising lawyer, said, "Who will come forward to marry me at the age of forty? I had to sacrifice the best part of my life to help my family". Nayana's father also was a lawyer. But he was not a successful practitioner and his earnings were not sufficient for the maintenance of the family. Nayana was the eldest of ther parents' six children — four daughters and two sons. Being the eldest of all, Nayana therefore realised the financial problems of her father. She resolved not to marry till the family income was adequate. After passing B.A. examination, she took a course in stenography and obtained a diploma in it. She was fortunate to be employed as a stenographer in a bank. But she did not like it since she had at times to work till late hours. She therefore wanted to change vocation and began to study for a degree in law in the eveining section of a nearby college. She eventually passed the final law examination and obtained the LL.B. degree. With her meagre income she had been meeting the expenses of engineering education of one of her brothers. He completed his studies and got a job. Nayana then resigned from her post of stenographer and started practice as a lawyer. Meanwhile, all her younger sisters got married. Regarding her own marriage, Nayana said, "After my sisters' marriage, I did not get any proposal for my own marriage. Thus I am now continuing my single life and busying myself in legal practice".

Renuka, 43, was the second of her parents' eight children, of whom five were daughters and three sons. All the sons were younger to the daughters. The father was an upper division assistant and could hardly maintain the family and give good education to all the children. The eldest daugher failed the matriculation and left the school. Renuka, the second daughter, passed matriculation and tried to do something for her poor family. Fortunately, she got a job of lower division assistant in a government office. She could thus support the education of her younger sisters and brothers and felt happy to see that they came out of colleges and university one after the other. When asked about her own marriage, Renuka said, "Instead of my own, I thought about the marriage of my elder sister. She also wanted to devote herself to looking after the younger sisters and brothers. So I had to take the responsibility of maintaining my unmarried elder sister, too. The other sisters and brothers got married in due course. I am happy to see their married life. But the time for me has already gone. Who will come to marry me at such a late age ?"

Rameswari was the youngest of her parents' seven children — six daughters and one son. Her brother, the only male in the family was a driver and he got duly married. But after his marriage he lived away from home in Karbi Anglong district and did not extend any help to the family. One elder sister of Rameswari lost her husband during her father's life time and she therefore came back to stay with her parents. When Rameswari's father dies, she had to take the responsibility of the widowed mother along with the widowed elder sister. She had no alternative than to seek for any job that came in her way. She secured a job as a weaver in a commercial weaving centre to earn for the family. Under these circumstances she could not think of marrying and refused the few marriage proposals that came.

ii *Chronic ailments and physical disabilities* :

A person who has a chronic health problem or happens to be physically handicapped is regarded as a sort of deviant in every society. These may give her a special status in society. A woman with a physical defect has considerable difficulty in getting married. Very often such a woman has to remain single. Not to speak of blindness, even ordinary defects which do not hamper a girl in her household duties stand in the way of her marriage. These are considered as disqualifications for a girl to get married. There are social prejudices in regard to these defects. Women with physical defects are often considered inauspicious. Lameness, deafness, squint eye, leucoderma, etc., have negative connotations for marriageability of a girl. Leucoderma often leads to isolation of the whole family from the rest of the villagers.

The cases cited here give an idea of how a physical defect leads to lifelong celibacy for a woman.

Durga, 37, belongs to a Brahmin family of a village of Kamrup district. She developed leucoderma at a tender age. The villagers excommunicated the whole family because of her ailment. Her feelings were deeply wounded, and with a view to saving the innocent family members from humiliation, she left the native village in 1968 for good at the age of 22 to stay at a home for destitute women in Guwahati. Such examples are to be found not only in the rural areas of Assam but also in the city. Dipa and Hiran are two single women aged 32 and 34, respectively. They were born and brought up in the city of Guwahati. Both of them have suffered from the same disease — leucoderma. They feel that they have no chance of getting married. They are working in government offices leading independent single lives.

Phuleswari, aged 30, said that she had a chest pain recurring since puberty. "I therefore did not get any marriage proposal. The people of my village also began to evade me for the disease. So I had to leave my native place in search of a job to carry my single life". This young woman is working as a polythene bag-maker in an industrial unit for earning her livelihood.

Parul has been blind in one eye from her childhood. She knew that she could not get married because of her blindness. So she came to the city for earning a living. She is working as a maid in a working women's hostel in Guwahati.

iii. *Loss of parents in childhood* :

To be an orphan in childhood is a great calamity. The kin who are sympathetic and well-off may look after an orphaned child. But when the near kin are poor, the future of an orphan is bleak and uncertain. Such orphans may never receive any education and usually have to struggle hard for mere survival. The fate of an orphaned girl may be even more difficult than an orphaned boy who has the prospect of becoming at least a day labourer. An orphaned girl of a poor family has hardly any chance to marry and has to remain single struggling somehow to maintain herself. Many such girls end up at the destitute home in the city.

Mina's mother died when she was only three months

old. Her father married again and the stepmother looked after her in her infancy. Her father also died soon after. Till she was 5 years old, her stepmother reared her up somehow. But she remembers that her stepmother treated her very badly. So Mina's maternal uncle took her to his house. Everything went well for about three years, but gradually her maternal uncle, who was very poor, began to feel her as a burden. He took her to Guwahati and kept her in a family as a maid-servant. She was treated well there, but when she attained puberty the family members did not like to take the responsibility of keeping her any more. Without a job and a shelter Mina saw darkness all around and ultimately landed herself into the destitute home. She is 36 years old.

Radha, 30, was only two years old when both her parents died. A co-villager gave her shelter. But the family was very poor. Gradually they began to feel her as a burden. When she was about 7 years, the head of the family took her to the destitute home. When asked about her marriage she said, "Who will come with a marriage proposal to the destitute home? I have had no chance to find a husband".

Jogalata became an orphan at the age of five. Her maternal uncle brought her up. The uncle, however, was very poor. When she grew up, she felt that she was a burden on the poor uncle. She knew that the uncle was not in a position to arrange her marriage. When she heard about the destitute home, she had a discussion with her uncle who gave consent to her to be admitted in it. On receiving his consent, she entered the home and has been staying there since. Now she occupies a supervisory position in the home itself. She is now 34 years old. She said : "As in my maternal uncle's house, so also in the destitute home, I have no opportunity to get married. But if I get a chance, I shall marry for the sake of my future security".

iv. *Unwed motherhood* :

Unwed motherhood is not common in Assam. In urban areas, such motherhood scarcely comes to light, since modern methods to overcome unwanted pregnancy are easily available and such occurrences are easily concealed. In rural areas these methods are beyond the reach of innocent villagers and an unwed mother has to accept the social consequence. The rural society does not condone such happenings and in an overwhelming number of cases an unwed mother has to remain unwed and single for ever.

In the rural areas, the unwed mother generally does not conceal the name of the male partner. It is found in the sample that the male partner tempted the girl with the prospect of marriage and after her conception, betrayed and refused to marry her. In some cases, the girl was violated against her will but when she conceived, the offender always denied any responsibility. In either case, it was the woman who suffered and had to remain unwed for good but the man escaped without having to pay any penalty.

> Sadari, 45, is a nurse who belongs to a Kayastha family of upper Assam. She fell in love with a patient who promised to marry her. They became acquainted with their respective families and were in very good terms with the family members. The man took liberties with Sadari, which resulted in her becoming pregnant. But when this was brought to the knowledge of the man, he refused to marry her. She did not go in for an abortion but delivered a baby. She resolved to rear the baby on her own and continued to work in the hospital. She has had to bear all the social stigma and did not ever think of marrying. She is staying with her child at the quarters allotted to her.
>
> Puspalata belonging to a village of south Kamrup, read up to Class VIII. She fell in love with a boy from the same village. They used to meet frequently. As a result of pre-marital intimacy, Pushpa conceived; but when the boy was informed about it by herself, he turned his back and refused to marry her. Puspa gave birth to a child and her parents' family was ex-communicated by the villagers. In order to remove the embarrassment of her poor peasant family, Puspa came to a destitute home with her child to stay there in 1979.
>
> Susama, Kalita by caste, hails from a village of Lakhimpur district. While studying in Class X, she developed a love affair with one of her teachers and she eventually conceived. She informed the teacher about her pregnancy but the teacher refused to marry her. She found herself in a very awkward situation and immediately left her village.

She came to the destitute home with her father, where she ultimately gave birth to a child. She has ever since been staying in the house with her child. She is 23.

Saraswati, a Brahmin woman belonging to a rural area of Kamrup, is an orphan. She was brought up by her maternal uncle. Once she visited her married sister's house and stayed there for about a month. Her sister's husband soon developed a fancy for her and took liberties with her. As a consequence she conceived, but tthe sister's husband did not confess his guilt. In shame and to overcome with guilt she left home and ultimately landed in a destitute home of Guwahati.

Champa, a Kalita woman, similarly conceived when the doctor who used to treat her, took liberties with her in his own chamber. Ultimately she had to take shelter in a destitute home, leaving her widowed mother at her village in Nagaon district. She read up to Class X.

Thus for various reasons outlined above, many women in the Assamese society have to remain unmarried and become a part of the category of single women along with widows and divorcees. The social horizon of these single women are discussed in Part Three.

PART THREE

SOCIAL HORIZON OF THE SINGLE WOMEN

8

LIVING ARRANGEMENTS

The Assamese Hindu society is characterised by patrilocal residence. A woman lives either in the parental house where her father is the head of household or with her husband. In the absence of her husband, she lives with her grown up son(s) as a dependent mother. But due to the new situation of single status, arising out of the different causes (mentioned in Part Two), she feels the necessity of having separate accommodation for herself. All single women have to face and cope with difficulties of finding accommodation. All such women irrespective of earlier life in joint family or nuclear family at the time of becoming single face similar problems.

The single women covered in this study had to arrange for suitable accommodation in different localities of the city. Consideration of security is a prime consideration since they have to live on their own or with very young children. The single women in the sample are found to have the following types of living arrangements : (i) own house, (ii) parental house, (iii) rented accommodation, (iv) allotted quarters, (v) hostel.

In this study, 'own house' covered not only a house built by the single woman herself, but also any house or apartment in the husband's premises, occupied by her from before the death of, or separation from, the husband. 'Parental house' implies the house belonging to parents, brothers, uncles or other consanguineal kin of the single women. 'Rented acommodation' means any house, or a part thereof, occupied on payment of monthly rent out of the income of a single woman but does not include allotted quarters provided by the employer or rooms in working women's hostels, even though rent may be paid for such accommodation. 'Allotted quarters' are house allowed to be occupied by the Government or any other employer either free of rent or on payment of rent at a rate which is usually much lower than the prevailing market rate. 'Hostels' include not only working women's hostel but also hostel specially constructed for helpless destitute women.

In the sample of 110 single women, 19 women are found to be living in their own house, 31 in parental houses, 20 in rented accommodation, 8 in quarters provided by the employer and 32 in hostels. Table 24 shows the details.

Table 24
Living arragements of single women in the sample

Living arrangements	*Widow*	*Divorcee*	*Unmarried*	*Total*	
				Number	*Per cent*
Own house	13	2	4	19	17.3
Parental house	10	6	15	31	28.2
Rented accommodation	4	9	7	20	18.2
Allotted quarters	7	-	1	8	7.3
Hostel	6	13	13	32	29.0
	40	30	40	110	100.0

Table 24 indicates that the majority (57.2 per cent) of the single women have living arrangements in parental houses and hostels. Many (28.2 per cent) women have taken shelter in the parental houses. Living arrangement in the parental house, which is the most natural possibility, is an index of the continuing importance of familial kinship in the Assamese society. It is the parental family which can provide help and succour to a single woman. In her parental family she can expect affection, understanding and support from her father and, in his absence, from her brothers. In the male dominated society, a single woman generally feels secure and protected in the proximity of her father or brothers. The proximity to siblings provide her with companionship and a sense of safety.

In the rural society, one comes across many instances of mainly widowed sisters living as dependents in their brothers' households. Next to her husband, her parents or brothers naturally are the best support to a single woman.

On the other hand, Table 24 shows that an equally high number (29 per cent) of single women are living in hostels. The hostels represent a substitute to the traditional kinship support created in the urban social context. In the absence of familial kinship support in the urban context, the women, many of whom are migrants to the city, have to take shelter in the protected environs of a hostel rather than rented accommodation. Here she finds a secure atmosphere because of the norms and regulations having a semblance to parental authority. She can also depend on the hostel authority for her protection in the adverse environment of the urban milieu. Because of this preference for hostels, there is a heavy rush for accommodation in such institutions. But there is a limit for admission into such institutions. For example, those whose income exceeds Rs. 1000.00 per month are not eligible for admission in one of those institutions.

On the other hand, it is not easy to make other living arrangements by the single women moving to the city. It is extremely difficult for a single woman to build her own house unless she is helped by her kin on either side and unless she has a regular and high income herself. Very often a widow inherits a house built by her husband. She might also build a house herself on a piece of land left by her husband or gifted by her father. But a divorcee rarely ever succeeds in getting a house built by her husband.

Similarly, it is very difficult to make living arrangement in rented accommodation. The rate of rent in the city is very high. Those single women who have been forced by the circumstances to make such an arrangement are found to be living in slums in unhygienic and insecure surroundings in the city.

To get quarters provided by the employer is a stroke of luck. Such arrangements do not come in the way of the majority of single women.

Some working single women have the good fortune of securing accommodation in working women's hostels. Majority of the women living in the hostels belong to the category who live in destitutes' hostels.

The general pattern of living arrangement is, therefore, veers round the two major categories, namely, parental houses and destitute homes (Fig. 9). The case materials on the different types of living arrangment illustrate the situation adequately.

Own house

To possess a house is the most satisfactory living arrangement for a single woman. Though it is difficult for a single woman to live on her own, she can find some kin to live with her for the sake of company and security. But most single women simply are not house-owners. Table 24 shows that only 17.3 per cent of the women have possessed houses of their own. Most of them belong to the categories of widows.

The widows whose husbands died young rarely have the opportunity to build houses. Elderly widows or widows in the higher income group often build separate houses. The majority of the women do not like to stay even in parental home after the death of their parents.

Table 24 shows that 13 out of 40 widows have their own houses. Some of them have continued to live in the houses constructed during the lifetime of the husband, some have completed the half-constructed houses of the husband, and some others have built houses with their own income on land gifted by the father or other members of the parental family. It is rarely that a widow can purchase a piece of land out of her own resources alone and build a house thereon.

There are instances where the widows have the good fortune of inheriting their husbands' houses.

> Senehi is a widowed wife of a lower division assistant. It was a permanent government job to her husband with a salary of Rs. 850.00 per month. He purchased a plot of land near his father's house in a suburban area of the city. By taking a loan from his office he constructed a modest house on that land. As his father's house could not comfortably accommodate all the members of the parental family, he and Senehi shifted to the newly constructed house. But Senehi's husband died about a month after their shifting. Senehi, however, has continued to live in the new house with her four children.

Monorama's husband was a headmaster of a lower primary school. He possessed two kathas of land on a hillock in the eastern fringe of the city and built a house thereon. She has been living in this after her husband's death.

Bimala, a widowed wife of a tax-collector and Bilati, another widowed wife of a fitter, have been living in modest thatched cottages built by their respective husbands on government land found in the city. Whether their husbands had occupied these plots by encroachment or on regular settlement basis could not be clarified by them. If the occupation was by encroachment, there is always the prospect of eviction.

Cases have been found where the widow has either constructed a house at her own expense on the land already acquired by the deceased husband during his life time or has completed the partly-built house after the death of the husband.

Bandana, a doctor, was married to a man who too was a doctor. They lived in a rented house in the city. Her husband purchased a plot of land in Guwahati; but before he could build a house, he died. Bandana continued to stay in the rented house for sometime. She had her own income from medical practice and also some savings. Using this along with the sale proceeds of the car she owned, she has constructed a house on the plot of land and shifted to live in the new house.

But Bharati, another widow has completed the partly-built house after her husband's death. Her husband was an accountant in a government office. He started to construct a house on family land in the same compound where his brothers lived and with whom she and her husband lived in a joint household. But her husband died before he could complete the house. Bharati received life insurance policy money of her huband to which she was the nominee. With this amount in addition to her income as a lower division assistant, she was able to complete the unfinished house. She received all help from her husband's brothers in completing this. She is now living in the new house with her 14 years old son. Her security is ensured because her husband's brothers have their houses in the same compound.

A widow can also construct a house of her own, if she fortunately acquires a piece of land by way of inheritance or gift from her parents. Two such cases have been cited here.

> Snehalata, a college teacher, belongs to a well-to-do family of the city. Being the original resident as well as a government officer, her father could acquire a big plot of land in Guwahati during the tenure of his service. On the death of her father, Snehalata inherited a share of the father's landed property in the city. She was married to a high government official and they were living in a town of upper Assam. When her husband died, her brothers took her to the parental home. Snehalata did not stay long in the parental home since she could construct a house with the money inherited from her husband on the land inherited from her father. Her brothers helped her in building the house and on its completion she shifted to live in the new house with her three children.

> Padumi's husband was an electrician and died by accidental electrocution in the course of this duty. She received due compensation from the electricity department. Her father brought her to live in the parental house in Guwahati. The father also gifted a plot of land to her in the same compound where the parental house stood. With the compensation she had received from her husband's employer, she constructed a small cottage on this plot of land and began to live there independently with her two sons and one daughter. She has been appointed as a peon in her husband's office on compassionate ground.

It is revealed by the cases that death may take away the husband, but the familial kin of the widow often come to her help. A widow may, further, be able to build a house on her own land left by the husband and by the money inherited from him. But a divorced woman has very little chance of being helped by her husband's family or of getting any land or money from her husband.

The problems of a divorced woman in respect of living arrangements are not the same as that of a widow. Assamese women are too shy and do not like to assert their rights in public after divorce or separation from husband. The practice generally is that a divorced woman leaves the husband's house without any fuss. She claims no share of the husband's landed property nor any money. Rarely does she go to the court to make any claim. As a result of all these, she cannot, generally have the means to purchase or build a house of her own. Only two out of the 30 women in the sample have possessed their own houses. But these two appear to be exceptions rather than reflect the prevalent rule.

> Niru is a highly educated divorced woman. She is a professor and draws a decent regular income. She made savings from her earnings with a view to building her own house. She purchased a small plot of land in the city and then constructed a moderately good house on it. Her case may be regarded as an exception.

In the Assamese Hindu society — characterised by patrilocal residence, patiarchal form of authority and patrilineal inheritance— the existence of an unmarried daughter beyond what is regarded as marriageable age creates tensions in the family, especially after the death of her father. Her status depends upon the attitude of her brothers and on the pattern of her relationship with her brothers' wives. It is therefore seen that after gaining economic independence they generally do not like to live as part of their married brother's households. They also try to make their own independent living arrangement.

It is, however, extremely difficult for an unmarried woman to acquire a plot of land and build a house of her own. It might be possible only at a late stage in life when she is economically well-established.

Only four women in the sample of 40 unmarried women live in their own houses. They have got the land as gift from their respective fathers. All of them are teachers and have some savings from their income. At the late ages of fifty or beyond, they have become able to construct houses of their own.

> Labanya, a dedicated unmarried teacher, had a small plot of land acquired as a gift from her father. She has built a small house on the plot from her own savings. It is a modest 'Assam-type' house with two small rooms and a kitchen. In constructing the house, she has got the help of

her married younger brother who lives in an adjacent house. She has kept one of his brother's sons, a student of class VII, with her. Labanya helps him in his studies and he also provides her with company and a sense of security. This has proved to be a satisfactory living arrangement for Labanya. She is 56.

Binaya, another unmarried teacher of 48, has a small house of her own (*see* p.159). It was gifted to her by her father, just before his death within the same compound of his house. She lives separately from the brothers who occupy the parental house. She gets help and co-operation from her brothers and brothers' wives. She, in turn, takes care of the study of her brothers' children.

Parental house

Parental house, as already mentioned, is the most natural place where a single woman ordinarily resides in the first instance. It is the obvious shelter for her. About 28 per cent of women in the sample are residing in their parental houses.

A young Assamese widow having no separate arrangement for continuing to live with the husband's family or having become unable to continue in the rented house after her husband's death, inevitably looks forward to her parents for shelter and maintenance. But when the parents are dead, the widow gradually begins to feel that she is a burden on the brother's family and tries for independent living arrangement. If she gets a job, and the economic conditions permit, she either builds a separate house for herself or arranges for separate living, supported by her own income.

Malika's husband, who was a superintendent of police, died young before they had any children. After her husband's death, she continued to live with her husband's parents and other family members. She said, "Though it was a joint family, I felt very lonely. I therefore discussed the matter with my parents and told them that I wanted to stay with them. Accordingly, my father took the permission of my in-laws and I came back with him to stay with my parents". Mallika's parents' house is in Guwahati itself. She is the only daughter of her parents' four children. Her brothers are living in their different working places outside the city. Her father is a reputed academician and a well-to-do person. With the help of her father by approaching the authority of a school, Mallika secured a job of a teacher in a high school. She is found happy to live with her parents.

But Dipika, another widowed wife of a medical officer, did not like to be a burden on her father and married brother in her parental family. At the time of her husband's death, Dipika and her husband lived in the official quarters at Tezpur. Her husband died leaving behind four children. She had to vacate the official quarters and had no other alternative than to move to her parental house. But dint of hard labour, she secured a good position in a competitive examination and got an executive job in a government department. Thereafter she began to feel herself as a burden on her parental family along with her four children. She discussed the matter with her father and brother and they appreciated her point of view. Her father, a retired government officer, constructed a separate room for her with a separate kitchen in the same house. Living in the same premises with her near kin, but with separate living arrangement, Dipika is happy with a feeling of security.

The cases of widows who at the same time happen to be the only child of their parents are slightly different. After having returned to live with the parents, they rarely think for a separate establishment. They usually get the necessary affection and sympathy of their parents besides economic and social security. The cases of Dipti, Ranjana and Binita are of this nature. They were brought back home by the parents soon after their widowhood. They have shared the same establishment and are living as members of the same parental family without thinking of separate residential arrangement.

Divorced and separated women also generally prefer to go back to parental home after separations. Like the widows, they also prefer this for reasons of security or for temporary shelter. If they have some independent source of income, they generally like to have independent living arrangement. Even childless women who are not a burden on the parents, especialy if they happen to be the only issue of their parents, display the same desire for independent living arrangement.

> Rumi, who read up to the post-graduate level, is a beloved daughter of an affluent father. She was given in marriage to a company executive staying in the same city. But the marriage broke down before she bore any child. Her father, a medical practitioner, brought her back to his house. Being the eldest child in the family, she was treated with kindness and affection by her younger brothers and sisters. She lived with them in comfortable and secure surroundings. But as she confided to the researcher : "would it be possible to live like this after the marriage of my brothers or when my parents are no more? I want to have separate living arrangement before my brothers get married".
>
> Gita, another divorcee, is the only daughter of her parents. She was born and brought up in the city and was a student of engineering course at the time of her marriage. But before completion of her study, she got married with an engineer by her own choice, who was senior student of the same college. She gave birth to a son after seven years of their marriage and she had a married life of about 8 years duration. The marriage broke down when the child was only one year old. Just before the separation they lived in a rented house. After separation, it was impossible for Gita to pay the house rent and also to look after the child. She had to come back to her parents. Being the only issue of her parents, accommodation was no problem for her and she was also received compassionately by her parents. Later on, Gita completed a condensed course of engineering, took a diploma in it and joined in a service as a junior engineer. But after being employed, Gita has felt for separate living arrangement as soon as possible. She said: "After continuing independently as a house-wife for about 8 years, I find it difficult to live as a dependent of my parents. I cannot arrange household things in my own way, I cannot cook independently and I cannot entertain my friends without mother's permission. I have no authority in the house at all". She wants to have living arrangement in a working women's hostel. But her son

would not be allowed to live there with her. Gita's problem has remained unsolved at the time.

The women, who returned to live with their parents, following dissolution of their marriages, said that it was only for protection and security that they returned to the parents. It is their considered opinion that to live with parents cannot be a permanent solution to their problem.

It is clear that parental house is not as congenial as is often thought to be. The parents may welcome a separated daughter back but the other members of the family may not share the same attitude as the parents have towards her. The causes of unwillingness of a woman to live permanently in a parental house, as found in the study are, mainly, due to difficulty of adjustment with other members of the parental family, actual negligence or fear of such negligence towards the divorced or separated woman after the death of the parents, and lack of say and authority in the management of family affairs.

It is obvious that unmarried women have no other place but the parental home. A widow may have her husband's house and a divorcee may, with savings accumulated during married life build their own houses; but an unmarried woman continues automatically to live in her parental house. There is no question of her leaving the parental home, unless circumstances compel her to leave. In the case of a widow or a divorcee, she returns to parents' home after having the experience of leading a different life. Such a woman may have already developed certain attitude and preferences and the slightest mal-adjustment may be sufficient for her to seek accommodation away from the parental house.

The case of an unmarried woman is different. She is accustomed to living in the environment of the parental house and cannot ordinarily think of leaving the house. Besides, she has not seen the outside world from the angle of vision of a married woman. She has not faced the hazards of a widow or a divorcee. For a never-married woman, the psychological provocation to leave the parental house is generally very much greater than in the case of a widow or a divorcee. It is therefore seen in Table 24 that majority (15) of the women, living in parental house, belong to the category of unmarried women.

But as found in the study, these unmarried women are not

always happy in their parental houses. The women, who are living with their unmarried brothers and sisters in parental houses have expressed fear as to what would happen after the brothers got married. The women, who have to live with their married brothers are not happy with their broihers' wives. But they have tried to stay with them for the sake of security, protection and avoidance of social criticism for living alone.

But the unmarried women, who have no brothers, are living in their parental houses without any complication. In the absence of a male issue in the family, they have to look after their aged parents with all the responsibilities. So these women do not think for a separate living arrangement for them.

Similarly, the women who have decided to remain unmarried in order to support their natal families do not think about a separate living arrangement leaving their parents and unmarried brothers and sisters. But they are prepared to live separately after their brothers' marriage if the situation so requires. Two cases have been cited here.

> Renuka, 43 years of age, is a lower division assistant in a government office. She has already started building her new house in the city by taking a house building advance from her office. She has heavy burden to bear with her ailing widowed mother, an unmarried elder sister and also the widowed wife of her deceased younger brother. She has another younger brother of marriageable age who is helping her in constructing the house. When asked regarding her separate living arrangement, Renuka replied, "I cannot move now to reside in my own house, because I have to look after ailing mother along with the other members of my family. I am making my house only for renting it out". Renuka intends to rent her house, so that the additional income from the rent enables her to maintain the family. She would continue to live in the parental house till circumstances compel her to leave it, as she reported.
>
> Uma, 48, is a superintendent of another government office (*see* pp. 163-64) . She has already built a house of her own with a loan and her savings. But she does not want to move into it. It is fetching good rent. She has the responsibility of looking after her widowed mother and two unmarried younger sisters. Uma's married younger

brother is also staying with her. She said : "I do not want to stay in my own house without a male member. My house is only a source of income for the family. But in future, I may move into my house if any problem arises in the family". She wants to stay in her parental house as long as possible.

Rented accommodation

The study reveals that the problems of arranging rented accommodation in the city are, mainly, due to non-availability of a house at reasonable rents within the financial capacity of a single woman, problem of suitable location, problem of security and distance of the house from place of work. Table 24 shows that 18.2 per cent of the women in the sample are living in rented accommodation found in the city.

Among the widows, only 4 respondents are residing in rented accommodtion. They are found to have been living in slum quarters in unhygienic conditions. All the houses are thatched huts and the accommodation is in the nature of single room without any conveniences.

It is difficult for a divorced woman to arrange suitable rented accommadation as she is generally not welcomed by the landlord. Of the 30 women belonging to this category in the sample, 9 are living in rented accommodation. But living in rented accommodation poses great problems to a single woman who is separated from her husband. A few cases with different problems have been discussed here.

Manimala, a double M.A., is a teacher of a higher secondary school. After her separation she stayed at the parental house along with her son for about one year and then she rented a house in a locality rather far away from her parents. "But I could not stay for long in that locality", she said. "In the mean time the agitation against the foreigners began in Assam. When the boys of the neighbourhood came to know about my unsympathetic views on the agitation, they started to pelt stones at my house at night and generally harassed me. It became a problem for me to stay in that locality", she added. Manimala eventually shifted to another rented house in a different locality.

Apati was deserted by her husband. Her husband left

her at his own house in a village of Kamrup district and did not return. She stayed in her husband's house for about a year depending on the kindness of her husband's married younger brother. But gradually she felt herself with her three children as a heavy burden on the husband's family. At last she left her husband's place with the consent of her in-laws to join in a power-loom-production centre as a weaver. After joining the service, she has arranged her accommodation, in a bare single room, in the city at a rent of Rs. 40.00 per month. "But this is not a proper arrangement for me and my children," she said. "I am not keeping my children with me. My younger brother has taken their responsibility and has kept them with him". Apati is unhappy without the company of her children. Her income is too small to bring them to live with her.

Uttara, a girl from rural area of lower Assam, got married without her parents' consent. But the husband, a taxi driver, deserted her after some time. She said, "In the absence of my husband, I had to leave the rented house where we lived together after marriage. I went to my parents harbouring the hope of staying with them. But my parents refused to keep me as I had married without their consent. Being helpless, I came to stay with a family in the city as a maid-servant. The family was known to me since my childhood and they were therefore very much sympathetic to me. After about a month, I got a job of a polythene bag-maker in a small factory in the city. Then I came to stay separately in a rented room near the factory with another woman working in the same factory". Uttara thus has tried to adjust with her living arrangement by sharing the rent of Rs. 30.00 per month between her and her mate. There is not much difficulty in her case as she has no issue. Childless women working in the same establishment find it easier to arrange a room on share basis. In addition to economic relief, living together with other women co-workers give a sense of security.

As we have already indicated, it is not easy for an unmarried single woman to arrange rented accommodation. In the sample, there are 7 (out of 40) unmarried women adjusting with such type of living arrangement. But they are mostly women belonging to higher income group who have come from outside the city in connection with their jobs.

> Padmini, 37, is a lawyer. She hails from a town of lower Assam. Her father had arranged a single room for her with a family known to him. She said, "My parents cannot leave the native house to stay with me. I have no brothers or sisters also to stay with me in the city. But I am not willing to stay alone in a rented house. So my father had made this arrangement for me. I am paying Rs. 150.00 per month for the room. There is no separate kitchen. I prepare my food in a corner of the same room. I have no separate toilet, too. I am sharing the same washing conveniences with my landlord. I am living in this way in a single room only for my security and protection".
>
> Bani, an unmarried school teacher is staying alone in a rented house at the age of 49. Her parents also live in Guwahati. But after her father's death she did not like to stay with the parental family, where her two married brothers live. Only to look after her widowed mother, she stayed in her father's house. She said, "My mother died last year. After her death, I did not feel the necessity of my presence in the family. So I decided to make separate living arrangement in a rented house. Fortunately, I got a small house near my school for Rs. 200.00 per month. I discussed the matter with my younger brothers and left my parents' house to live separately. Now I feel happy with my living arrangement. My brothers and their wives occasionally come to see and help me".

Allotted quarters

It is not easy for women employees to secure quarters provided by the employer. In the sample, only 7.3 per cent of women could secure accommodation in allotted quarters.

When a widow is given employment on compassionate ground in the same office where her husband had worked, she is provided with quarters by the employer in case her husband had been living in one provided by the employer. But she cannot claim the same house. Her employment depends on her educational qualification and her suitability for a post falling vacant at the time. In general it is found in the sample that the widows have lower educational qualifications than their husbands and so they are absorbed in lower posts which are in conformity with their lower educational qualifications. Having been employed in lower posts than their husbands, they are not entitled to continue to live in the same houses as they did during their husband's lifetime. As the job status is lower than that of the husband, the type of house to which, the widow is entitled is also inferior. At first the widow feels a little discomfort but later she regards it as a boon to have a house in a city like Guwahati at a low rent. All the women in the sample expressed satisfaction at being provided with quarters this way.

> Indira's husband was a lecturer. After his death she was appointed as a library assistant in the same educational institution. She had to shift from the lecturer's quarters to a house built for an assistant. Kuntala's husband was the superintendent in a government office. After his death, she was appointed as a record-arranger, and she moved into a new house meant for a lesser rank.
>
> The same was the case with Anima. Her husband was an upper division assistant in an office. On month after her husband's death, she was appointed as a lower division assistant in the same department. Regarding the adjustment in her allotted quarters, Anima reported, "Formerly we had a much bigger house than the present one. After my joining in the office, I had to leave the quarters allotted in my husband's name and had to come to stay in this small house allotted to me." As she informed she felt a little uneasy at first, but became gradually used to it.
>
> But Purnima's case is different. She is a medical officer of the State Government, when her husband died. She had quarters appropriate to her rank.

It is thus seen that the type of quarters allotted to a widowed employee depends on the qualification of the widow but not on the employment status and qualification of the deceased husband. On the other hand, all the women who are residing in quarters got accommodation and job on compassionate ground. Among the three categories of single women, only the widows could receive such considerations.

Divorced or separated women do not get such opportunity of getting allotted quarters. In the sample, none of these women is found living in quarters provided by the employer. The reason is that even if the husband might have been provided with such quarters, after divorce or separation, the husband continues to live in the allotted quarters while the wife has to leave it. Even if such non-working woman is given a job, it is generally not easy for her to get separate quarters.

Quarters provided by the employer is rare for unmarried women. In the sample of 40, only one woman has been found living in quarters provided by the employer. She is a hospital nurse and has a baby. It is due to the nature of her job that she is given such accommodation. Nurses everywhere are provided with quarters by the hospital authorities.

Hostel

Table 24 shows that out of 110 women in the sample as many as 32 (29 per cent) are living in hostels. They are mostly separated and unmarried women. The term 'hostel' covers two different types of accommodation: (i) hostel for working women and (ii) hostel for destitute women.

i. *Hostel for working women* :

During the period of field-work, there are only two hostels in the city for Hindu working women. One of them was a private organization to provide accommodation to about fifteen working women in a private residence in the eastern part of the city. The other hostel, known as *Mahila Nivas,* is run by a voluntary organization called *Yuva Nivas Santha.* The present study covered this hostel which provided accommodation to 53 working women during the period of investigation. It is a registered institution established in 1967. It is situated at Narengi, in the eastern part of Guwahati. The hostel is funded by donations received from individuals and grants-in-aid from the Board of Social Welfare of Central and State Government and other institutions and organizations. The Government of Assam have allotted a 10 bigha plot of land to this institution for the construction of two double-storeyed residential buildings for 300 working women, one residential building for 100 semi-educated women, a craft-training-cum-sales centre, a library, an auditorium, a health-centre with a nursing home, etc., for the residents of *Mahila Nivas* (Miri, ed. 1975 : 206).

A working single woman, especially an unmarried woman, is accommodated in this hostel on payment of rent. The rent is modest but the woman enjoys considerable security. The rent is remitted in case the working woman is an employee of the hostel.

Besides, this hostel had provided accommodation to 15 destitute women at the time of investigation. They were in 15-45 years age range and hailed from the rural areas of Assam. In the case of destitute women, no rent is realised and they have to be maintained by the hostel authorities. They have, of course, to work for the hostel and are trained for different jobs. They are paid small allowances for personal expenses.

ii. *Hostel for destitute women* :

There is one hostel for destitute women in the city, called *Home for Destitute Women and Helpless Widows*, situated at Jalukbari in the western fringe of Guwahati. This home was established in 1964-65 by the Government of Assam. The main object of this home is to help destitute women by giving shelter and opportunity to find out ways of livelihood. There is a training-cum-production centre in the home where the inmates get training in various crafts like sewing, weaving, doll-making and leather work. The training helps in their rehabilitation to a great extent. During the perioid of investigation (in 1981) there were 57 inmates in this home, of whom 16 had not yet attained the age of majority.

The distressed women of all the three categories, have no alternative but to come to the hostel for destitute women from the rural areas of Assam. Their parents, siblings and affines could not or would not support them. They gradually lose their ties with relatives. Each of them becomes a lone individual with no kin to look for support and help. For them the tranquil village life is a thing of a past. Within the four walls of the hostel, they have now to follow the rules and regulations of the institution and adhere to a disciplined code of day-to-day life prescribed by the authority. Their life is one of routine and monotony without much to look forward to in future. As a consequence, many of them lose finer feminine qualities. Many such single women show a sullen temper.

Nevertheless, the large number of women living in hostels, indicates that 'hostelry' is one of the major support systems created by urban society as a substitute of traditional kinship base.

9

THE WORK SITUATION

In the traditional Assamese society, a woman's position is conceived essentially as that of a dependent in which her basic needs of shelter, food and clothing are to be provided by her parents or husband. When she loses her parents or husband, she has to face the problem of economic security and alternative arrangements on these fronts. If she has children, there is then the additional responsibility of maintaining and bringing them up. Under the pressure of economic necessity, a single woman has to be a worker and an earner in the changed circumstances.

Most of the unmarried women have to work for their livelihood or to support their poor parental families without entering into matrimony (see Chapter 7). Among the widows and the divorcees in the sample of 110 women, only 5 widows and 4 divorcees were employed before becoming single. Thus, most of the women (68.2 per cent) in the sample were employed at the time of becoming single. They were essentially housewives engaged in domestic chores and in bringing up children. They were therefore dependent on their husbands' earnings.

A woman confined to household duties and responsibilities has to come out of the home environs in search of work on becoming single. Women constituting 58.2 per cent of the sample had to come to the city from different places of Assam in search of livelihood and accommodation. Tables 16.1, 16.2 and 16.3 (see Chapter 4) show the pattern of migration of these women. Urban-industrial development of Guwahati has created opportunities of various jobs for these women. The job opportunities act as the pull factor on them to come to the city from different parts of Assam to seek succour and relief. Of the total 64 immigrants in the sample, a large number (47) of women have come from the rural areas of Assam, while only 17 women have come from towns in search of livelihood in the city. Figure 8 shows the pattern of migration in the sample.

The compelling economic necessity has tended to weaken the traditional role of being just a housewife and adopt a new role as a worker in the changed circumstances. It is difficult for a housewife, who was always dependent on the husband or husband's decision to re-orient and organise herself in a new role and also to the new environment of her work situation. A smooth and orderly domestic setting is important for the welfare of her children while commitment at the place of work is essential for security and recognition in the service life. To keep a balance between the demands of her domestic life and work life is a problem arising out of her single status.

Help and co-operation in securing job

On becoming single, widows and divorcees suddenly come face to face with the grim realities of life. The unmarried women on the other hand get some time to prepare themselves for such a situation. The widows and the divorcees have to secure some job quickly for their own as well as their children's maintenance. It is, however, not easy for a widowed or a divorced woman to get a job quickly. For this, her kinsfolk usually come to her help to a considerable extent. In the sample, nearly 58 per cent of the single women have been helped by their kinsfolk. Table 25 shows the nature and extent of kinship help and co-operation in securing employment. Consanguineal kin provide such help most often (51.8 per cent). This is so since in the Assamese society the maintenance of unmarried, divorced or even young widowed women is considered to be the responsibility of the parents.

Table 25
Kinship help and co-operation in securing jobs

	Widow	*Divorcee*	*Unmarried*	*Total*	
				Number	*per cent*
Consanguineal kin	22	13	22	57	51.8
Affinal kin	5	2	-	7	6.4
Friends	7	4	4	15	13.6
Self-effort	6	11	14	31	28.2
	40	30	40	110	100.0

While the unmarried women usually live with the parents, the divorced and the widowed women also come to the parents at the first instance. The parents later on arrange for their employment wherever possible. It is for this reason that more than half of the women in the sample are found to have been assisted by the consanguineal kin. A few cases are cited below :

> Dipika, a widowed mother of four children, had studied up to post-graduate level before her marriage. After her husband's death, she had to come back to her parents' house. Dipika's father and brother encouraged and assisted her in appearing for the Assam Civil Service Examination in which she came out successful. She was appointed as a magistrate and posted in the city. She not attends to her work while living with her brother's family.

> Kalyani, a childless widow, was encouraged by her father to study law after her husband's death. Her father, a lawyer, helped in her studies and subsequently established her in a legal practice.

In the Assamese society, parents always play an active role in giving support not only to a widow, but also to a divorced or separated daughter.

> Niru was only a matriculate at the time of her divorce. Her parents encouraged and helped her to study up to Master's degree level. She then succeeded in getting a lecturer's job in a college.

In the emerging middle-class context of the Assamese society, education is considered essential for the economic security of the women. Besides supporting studies, the parents usually extend support to their dependent daughters in other ways. The father, especially, strives hard to see that his daughter is able to stand on her own during his life time. For instance, Mayatara, an unmarried woman 44, was appointed as a clerk with the help of her father in the same office where he worked.

Table 25 shows that an equal number (22) of widows and unmarried women received help from consanguineal kin in securing jobs.

Affinal kin, extending help to single women in securing jobs account for only about 6 per cent in the sample. Only 5 widows and 2 separated women received help from their affinal kin. Widowed women like Sarumai, Basanti and Lakhimi who hail from the villages of lower Assam were helped by their deceased husband's family members. They are employed as peons in their respective husband's offices.

It is found that about 13 per cent of single women in the sample received help from friends in obtaining jobs in the city. About 28 per cent of the women, however, secured employment through their own efforts. This was possible because they had the required educational qualifications. For the educated women, it is not very hard to get jobs since they are familiar with the procedures of application, interview and written examination.

The difficulties are more for illiterate women and women with limited education. Rameswari, an unmarried woman of 38, and Rohini, a separated woman of 35, thus had to satisfy themselves with humble jobs as weavers. They had to personally approach the owners of weaving factories for securing the jobs.

Nature of employment

The single women whether literate or illiterate, try to be economically independent by taking up various occupations available in the city. They generally find employment in 'women-centred' occupations in educational institutions, hostels for working women, weaving centres and hospitals. Women, employed in offices and industrial units, represent a new trend in Assam.

The fairly large number (28) of working women in the sample, engaged as teachers in different educational institutions (see Table

14), reflects the literacy level of Assamese womenfolk. Depending on their educational level, the women are employed as teachers in lower primary or high and higher secondary schools. Some single women possessing higher educational qualifications are engaged as college and university lecturers.

Employment in the teaching sector is not a new phenomenon in the Assamese society. The nature of work and venue suit the women most. Besides providing a source of livelihood, teaching offers the prospect of status in society. The peaceful atmosphere prevailing in the educational institutions and the vacation facilities attract the women to teaching.

The Assamese women are also gradually moving into other occupations, e.g., office jobs. Besides office jobs of upper division assistant, lower division assistant and typist, there are a few who worked as engineers. In such jobs, they work alongside men. For those without enough education, the office peon's job has become a new field of employment. Generally the widow of a peon is employed in the same establishment on compassionate ground. The sample consists of 9 such widows employed as peons.

Medical profession too has attracted a number of women. Nursing represents another emerging field. There are two widowed doctors in the sample. Women employees in nursing are found in considerable number. Most of them are unmarried women below the age of thirty with the possibility of marriage. There is one unmarried woman of 45 in the sample employed as nurse in a hospital.

Single women are also engaged in women's hostels, as matron or superintendent or in cooking, cleaning and sweeping jobs. The main reason for their choice to work in such hostels are the prospects of secured shelter and accommodation.

Some women are engaged in jobs in small-scale production centres. There are 9 weavers in the sample. Weaving is a traditional female occupation in the Assamese society. They are working in power-loom production centres in the city. Polythene bag-making is a new employment for a few women. But these jobs do not offer much security.

In the traditional Assamese society there are prejudices against women working in certain occupations considered not respectable for high-caste women. The nursing, sweeping, hair dressing and the like were taboo for high caste women. But in the new urban circumstances, such vocations are no longer considered 'closed' to the women of any caste. In fact, caste does not any longer appear to be related to the nature of jobs. Sadari, an unmarried Kayastha woman is found working as a senior nurse in a hospital. In another case, Sobha, a divorcee, is engaged as a hair-dresser in a beauty parlour. She also is a Kayastha by caste.

Income and expenditure

How far does job help a woman in playing her role as a bread-winner has been examined, to see her adjustment to the new situation. For this purpose, as outlined in Table 26, income has been classified under three broad headings — low, middle and high.

Income below Rs. 600.00 per month has been classed as low income, between Rs. 600.00 and 1200.00 as middle income and above Rs. 1200.00 as high income group. Each group has again been divided into three slabs, the detailed of which has been given earlier in Table 15. The income pattern of single women is also shown in Figure 10.

Table 26

Income group of single women in the sample

Income group	*Widow*	*Divorcee*	*Unmarried*	*Total*	
				Number	*Per cent*
Without income	3	7	5	15	13.6
Low income	22	12	9	43	39.0
Middle income	10	10	20	40	36.5
High income	5	1	6	12	10.9
	40	30	40	110	110.0

It is seen in Table 26 that only about 10 per cent of the women belong to the high income group. This group includes college and university teachers, officers, engineers, lawyers and doctors.

About 36 per cent of the women are in the middle income group. This group consists of high-school teachers, lower division assistants, upper division assistants, junior engineers, matrons and so on.

It is seen that 39 per cent of the women belong to the low income group. These women are employed as teachers in Montessory or lower primary schools, junior clerk, peon, weaver, polythene bag-maker, cooks, maids and so on.

It is further revealed that there is a concentration of widows and divorcees in the low income group while the unmarried women predominate the middle income group. It is difficult to deduce any sociological principle out of this phenomenon; but it is clear that the widows and the divorcees are always at a disadvantage in securing good jobs in their late age. The unmarrieds are always in a better position than women in the two other categories.

Table 26 further shows that 15 women are without income, living as inmates in the destitute homes. Among them, 8 are illiterate and this forecloses their options for employment elsewhere. Of the remainder, one woman has education up to lower-primary level, 3 up to middle-school level and another 3 up to high school level. But they too are tied up as inmates of destitute homes.

Expenditure pattern is closely linked up to one's social and economic position. Hence the pattern of expenditure differs from woman to woman according to different earning and class and other social considerations. Table 26 indicates that more than 52 per cent of the women in the sample face great hardship due to their poor earnings.

Besides routine expenditure on food, clothing and items of daily necessities, house rent is a major expenditure for the single women who have to live in rented accommodation.

> Hemanti, a primary school teacher, earns to Rs. 695.00 per month. She has to pay an amount of Rs. 150.00 per month as rent for a single room. She was separated from her husband after the birth of a child (*see* p 148).
>
> Apati, another separated woman and mother of three children, has been employed as a weaver in a weaving centre in the city. Her job is on contract basis and she earns approximately Rs. 150.00 per month as her renumeration. She pays Rs. 40.00 per month for her rented accommodation out of her limited income. She has not been in a position to keep the children with her due to her meagre earning and limited accommodation. Her children are being looked after their maternal uncle in the village (*see* pp 189-90).

A single woman living in a working women's hostel has to pay her hostel dues. Those who live in allotted quarters have likewise to pay house rent though in such cases the rents are not exorbitant.

A single woman who lives in her parental house, usually contributes an amount in cash or kind for the household expenditure. Thereby she tries to reduce her dependence status in the household.

> Gita, a divorcee, has been living with her parents along with her only child. She is a newly appointed junior engineer with a salary of Rs. 900.00 per month. She contributes Rs. 300.00 per month to her mother for household expenditure. Gita is the only issue of her fairthy well-to-do parents (*see* pp 184-85).

Seeking to uphold an independent status in the parental family by a working woman through contributing an amount to the household coffers is a new trend in the Assamese society. A single woman has thus to give much importance to the management of her accommodation.

> Bharati, a lower division assistant, is a widow living in her own house. Regarding her expenditure on household management, she said : "Though I am living in my own house, I have to spend money frequently on its repair and maintenance. I am now saving money from my monthly salary for earth-filling in my compound before the next monsoon". Relating to her other expenditure for living arrangement, Bharati further said : "Before my husband's death, I did not know about the payments of electricity bill, municipal tax, land revenue, etc. He always attended to these tasks. Now I have to manage all these from my limited income". She has been working since her marriage. So after the death of her husband, expenditure had to be drastically curtailed.

Next to accommodation, the expenditure of a single woman includes the maintenance of school going children, when she has children. This is quite heavy, especially for those whose children are being educated in private, English-medium schools.

> Narrating the expenses on her children, Bakul, a divorced mother, said : "The entire amount of Rs. 900.00

> which I get from my house as rent, is spent on the education of my three children. The school expenditure is quite heavy as they are studying in a private missionary school. Besides, they are also taking music and swimming lessons for which I have to pay an extra amount from my own salary". Bakul is a college teacher who gives priority to her children's education.

Savings and investments

Saving depends upon the levels of income and expenditure. If the income is small it goes in procuring the bare necessities of life. Even at higher income levels, saving is motivated by thoughts for future security and the desire to help the children in future. In the sample, only 41 per cent of women are found to have some savings or investments. Savings are generally kept in bank or invested in land, house, insurance and gold-ornament.

The women in the low-income group are seldom left with any money to save. Only 4 out of the 43 single women in the low-income group have some savings in banks. All of them are widows. A widow often receives an amount from the life insurance policy of her deceased husband or from his service benefits in the shape of provident fund, gratuity, etc.

> Indira, a library assistant, has received an amount of rupees fifty thousand as a nominee of her deceased husband's life insurance policy. Her husband was a university lecturer. Indira has invested this amount as a fixed deposit in a bank.

Most women who are able to save belong to the middle income group. Of the 40 women in this group (Table 26), 29 have some sort of savings. Most of them have invested their savings in purchasing land and constructing houses. Binita, a widowed school teacher, has contructed a house of her own on the plot of land left by her husband.

> Labanya, an unmarried school teacher, has acquired a plot of land as a gift from her father. She built a house thereon from her own savings. She has invested her savings in her late age. She is 56 (*see* p. 181).

> Only three women, namely Bharati, Anima and Malati, has been found in the middle-income group who

have kept their savings in fixed deposit in banks. Bharati, a lower division assistant, has a fixed deposit or rupees twenty five thousand, which she received as a nominee of her deceased husband's insurance policy.

Anima, who is also a lower division assistant, got an amount of rupees five thousand from her deceased husband's service benefits. She has invested the amount as a fixed deposit in a bank.

Four women, belonging to middle-income-group, have taken up insurance policies as a form of saving. Minakhsi, a widowed school teacher, has an education policy of rupees fifteen thousand for the future eduction of her son. Bakul, a divorcee and college lecturer, has also taken up an insurance policy for the security of her three children.

The study reveals that insurance is not very popular among the unmarried Assamese women. Ila, 34, an unmarried engineer said : "Insurnce money will be of no benefit to me. I am not interested in insurance policy". None of the unmarried single women in the sample has gone in for insurance as a form of investment for the future. The widows and the divorcees also feel that it is irksome to make regular payments of instalments. The unmarried women belonging to higher income group prefer to invest their savings in gold-ornaments. The traditional pattern of saving of Assamese women still prevails in the urban context. They feel that the gold-ornaments are more valuable than any other form of personal property. Besides, the gold-ornaments are more liquid and can be easily converted to cash in case of need.

Job satisfaction

What sort of satisfaction and women derive from work and the nature and extent of their adjustment in the new work situation are aspects worth looking into. The study shows that the single women are often compelled by the circumstances to take up jobs in a hurry. They have no choice and accept whatever employment comes their way. This is usually the position of a widow or a divorced woman. It is thus found that many single women, particularly those in the lower-income group, have very little scope for exercising preference in the employment field.

The widows, who are appointed as peons after husbands'

death have had no option to exercise. The women who are in the destitute homes have come there having no other choice or prospect.

Women who earn their livelihood by cleaning, sweeping, weaving, making polythene bags and doing similar jobs are not at all satisfied with their work. Their services are temporary and usually on contract basis. Their services may be terminated at short notice at any time. Their earnings too are meagre and hardly enable them to maintain themselves and their dependents. They work under considerable stress and anxiety.

> Sashi, a childless widow of 46, has been working as a superintendent of a working girls' hostel. But her post is purely temporary. Her pay is only Rs. 250.00 per month, though she is entitled to free food and lodging. She is worried about her temporary job and ever haunted by the fear of termination of her service.

There are two Ashram Sevikas in the low-income-group. These women have voluntarily accepted the life of social service and the renumerations they get are nominal. But they have high job satisfaction. They have dedicated their life to the work they do.

In the middle income as well as in the high-income groups, teaching seems to be the most favourite occupation among single women. Even in the low-income group, teaching job is found to be the first preference. Single women as teachers are found at all the levels of education from lower primary to the university. The reasons for this preference has already been indicated. They also derive considerable psychological satisfaction from teaching. Association with young boys and girls satisfies their maternal instinct. Love and respect which they get in the job compensate the poor salaries. They also feel more secure because the work environment involves no job hazard.

> Rumi, a childless divorced woman, is a Montessory school teacher earning a meagre salary of Rs. 350.00 per month. She is, however, happy with her job. She said : "I like to pass my time in the school. I find pleasure by singing the rhymes together with my tiny-tot students. I feel happy amidst the innocent children and forget my past".
>
> Bani, an unmarried woman of 49, is also a dedicated teacher in another Montessory school. She had Montes-

> sory training in Ahmedabad. She said : "I fell happy to see the smiling faces of the little boys and girls". Nilima, an unmarried graduate woman, is an assistant teacher of a high school. Instead of searching for any other job with better emoluments and advantages, she has taken the degree in B.T. to dedicate her life to teaching.

The single women teaching in colleges and university are also satisfied with their jobs.

Work environment

Work environment, conditions of work, transport facilities, hours of working and the like have considerable influence in the selection of jobs by a single woman. She has to be always cautious about the behaviour and attitude of male colleagues and superiors. It is found that sometimes the boss wants to take undue advantages.

> Nayana, an unmarried woman of 40, had to work as a stenographer to a young boss. But she did not like her job due to the tendency of her boss to take undue advantage. She had to work sometimes till late hours with him. She therefore wanted to change vocation and began to study for a degree in law. After obtaining the L.L.B. degree, Nayana resigned from her post of stenographer and has started practice as a lawyer.

> Phaguni, a widow of 22, came from a village to work as a book-binder in a press in the city. But the boss gave her trouble by his unseemly behaviour. She had to ultimately resign the job and became a polythene bag-maker in an industrial firm.

Distance is another factor which has operated as a handicap to the working women. A woman whose venue of work and residence are separated by several kilometres have to face a number of problems. She has to walk some distance for catching the bus. The bus again is always overloaded in the city and she may have to go standing among the total strangers. After office hours her return home may be delayed due to the distance she has to cover. If she returns to her lodging too late, it would be a subject for gossip among her neighbours. Many women in the sample have their work-centres far away from their place of residence in the city.

> Mayatara, an office assistant, lives in the southern part of the city while her office is in the extreme west. The distance between the two places by road is not less than twelve kilometres.

> Rameswari, another unmarried woman, is a weaver in a weaving factory in the Industrial Estate located in the east of the city. But she lives in the western part, about seven kilometres from her place of work.

Many other single women face similar difficulties of distance. Those who have children, have to suffer from the additional factor of worry.

Adjustment of work life

The single woman has to adjust herself with the new role of working woman as well as the authority of a family. She has to take equal responsibility of her work life and family life with her own decision. A few cases have been cited below to see the role of their adjustment in working life.

> Senehi, a widow, who studied up to class nine has got the chance to be appointed as a record arranger in a Government office, where her husband was a clerk. She has two sons and two daughters. Regarding her adjustment in service life, Senehi said : "I felt shy to come to the office for the first few days. It was also a problem for me to come to the office from a distance of about six kilometres, leaving my little children alone. So I had to keep my unmarried brother and sister in my house to look after my children during my absence. But I was torn by anxieties and hardly got any satisfaction in the job as such. I went on working mechanically". Senehi has now adjusted to her work situation.

> Tarami, a widowed mother of five children was appointed as a peon in her husband's organization (the Railways) where he was a fitter. Narrating her experience of the first few days of her working life, she said : "I was appointed in 1968. At that time women were gradually not appointed in such posts. After joining, I felt shy to move from table to table in the office taking files from one man to another. Later on, I adjusted myself to the job. To adjust in my working life, I had to stop my eldest daughter from

going to school so that she could look after my four other children during my absence. Instead of sending to school I tried for the marriages of my three daughters after they attained puberty".

Aghuni, another widow with four grown-up daughters, was appointed as a peon in her husband's office where he was a working as a *Khalasi.* She reported her problems of adjustment in the following way : "I had to come to work leaving my daughters alone. One day, on return from work in the evening, I found that my eldest daughter of seventeen years had eloped with a young boy to get married in the Kamakhya temple. But it was too late for me to go to the temple in search of my daughter. Next morning they came to me for my blessings and I was compelled to accept them. The boy was working in a motor garage without sufficient income. I therefore did not like to give my consent to their marriage. So, in my absence, they had taken the opportunity. After that I decided to keep my three other daughters with some good families as maid-servants".

These are the cases of uneducated women belonging to low-income group. The nature of adjustment differs in the case of educated women. An example of an educated woman is cited below :

Anima, graduate and widowed mother of three children, was immediately appointed in the office of her deceased husband. Her husband was an upper division assistant and she was appointed in the post of a lower division assistant. Recollecting the first day of her working life, Anima said : "I was weeping in the morning and tried to console myself. I knew that the job was the most important thing at the time for the upbringing of my children. But I felt uneasy to go out of the house with appearance of a widow. Leaving the house in the white dress of the widow without vermillion mark on the forehead and ornaments was a painful experience for me for first few days. I had also to think of the children during my duty hours. My first child, a son, was aged six years and the other two, daughters, were two years and one month old, respectively, at the time of their father's death. I had to keep one of

> my unmarried sisters with me to look after my young children. I also tried to visit my quarters during the lunch break of the office hours to see them. Now I have passed three years with the help of my unmarried sister. My sister has stopped her study after she failed the matriculation examination. She is looking my children. But after her marriage, I have to manage somehow".

All the women, mentioned above, are widows. They were appointed on compassionate grounds, in various establishments where their husbands worked. As they had to come out of their homes to take up jobs rather suddenly, they have had little time to prepare themselves for the new life pattern. Like their new working environment, they have to face a new situation on the domestic front by leaving the children along during working hours outside. In the changed situation of nuclear family-centred life, a single woman has to cope with the absence of kin help and co-operation to run her home smoothly. Senehi and Anima, as mentioned above, had to keep their unmarried brother and sister as long as possible, to look after the children during the office hours.

> Pankaji, a widow, who is working as a junior clerk, has adjusted to her new situation by employing a maid-servant to look after her little daughter. In this city, proper arrangement of creche for the children of working mother is not yet found.

10

THE SOCIAL AND CULTURAL CONTEXTS

The support of familial and other kin has always been of vital importance to individuals in the Assamese society. In day-to-day life as well as in situations of crisis, an individual always looks upon his or her parents, siblings and other kin for support and co-operation. Such reliance on family and kinship is more pronounced in the case of women than men because of the women's dependent status in the traditional society. For instance, it has been a widely prevalent practice for married women to come to their parental home for the birth of at least the first child and post-parturition convalescence. This apart, the links between a married woman and her parental family are kept warm and alive through visits to and extended stays at parental home.

The familial relatives offer a single woman with potential source of support in her changing situation. Her social relations are based on the nature of her adjustments to the new role. These have, therefore, to be examined carefully to understand the role of the family as well as kinship structure as a whole in relation to a woman who acquires single status.

Patterns of family and household

The changes in the pattern of family plays an important role in the case of single women. Lowie's (1966 : 215) observations on this aspect may be quoted here : "The death of husband or wife destroys the family; the marriage of a son or daughter alters its constitution, and so does anyone of a series of institutional regulations or of individual occurrences. A young widow who rejoins her parents can hardly be excluded from membership in the family". The termination of a marriage through death is itself a change in the pattern of family organization. Widowhood thus affects a woman's family and her social relations. The same is the case with a woman, divorced or separated from her husband. An unmarried woman in the Assamese society is generally not expected to leave her parental family till her marriage. A spinster lives mostly as a member of the joint family-centred household till making some alternative arrangements.

Table 27
Family pattern of single women in the sample

Pattern of family	*Widow*	*Divorcee*	*Unmarried*	*Total*	
				Number	*Per cent*
Denuded nuclear family	23	5	3	31	28.2
Joint family establishment	4	4	16	24	21.8
Extended family-centred household	5	2	2	9	8.2
No specific pattern	8	19	19	46	41.8
	40	30	40	110	100.0

Table 27 shows the distribution of single women in the sample in different types of family, organized after being single to adjust with their changed situations. A majority (28.2 per cent) of women in this study belongs to denuded nuclear families. Most such women are widows. Women making up 21.8 per cent of the sample still belong to the joint family-centred households. Most of them are unmarried women who have followed the traditional norm of the Assamese society by living with parents and siblings in joint set- ups. Some (8.2 per cent) of the women belong to extended family-centred households.

A large number (41.8 per cent) of the women does not belong to any organised pattern of family. They live alone and on their own in rented accommodation, hostels, homes for destitutes or in houses owned by themselves. The nature of social relations of single women in the different types of family and household arrangements are outlined below :

In the present study, nuclear family denotes a group consisting of a woman and her unmarried children. It is, in fact, a denuded nuclear family-centred household. The woman is usually a widow or a divorcee. So the emergent family is centred round her in her role as a mother. This sort of denuded nuclear family may also be termed as 'matri-centric'.

Such matri-centric nuclear family households are found mostly among the widows. It is seen that 37.5 per cent of the widows were members of joint households before the death of their respective husbands. After the death of a male member in a joint family it becomes the duty of the rest to look after the widow and children of the deceased person. But it is evident from the data that the joint family system is disintegrating and there is a trend towards nuclear family-centred households.

After being employed as a clerk Pankaj, a widow, has started her new kitchen in a corner of her room in her deceased husband's joint establishment. In Assames society, the cooking arrangement is separated first to form a nuclear family-centred household. By separating the kitchen she has formed the basis for a matri-centric nuclear family with her two-year old daughters. Thus she is living independently though in the same house.

Many respondents had to come out of their respective husbands' families and kingroups in search of new adjustments in the changed socio-economic circumstances of single status. On securing some means of livelihood, 57.5 per cent of the total widowed respondents have formed independent establishments. Majority of them have their own houses where they are living with their children. Many single women, living in parental houses also arrange separate establishments by having independent kitchens.

Nandita stays in a part of her father's house. She is a widowed

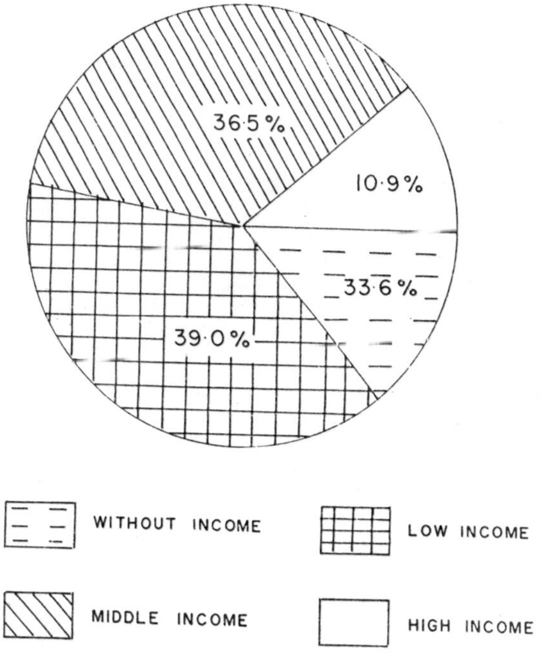

FIGURE 10. PATTERN OF INCOME OF SINGLE WOMEN IN THE SAMPLE

school teacher and a mother of two children — one daughter and one son, aged 8 and 2 years, respectively. She has made a separate living arrangement for her and the two children with a separate kitchen. She is thus not a dependent of her brother's household who too lives in the parental house. Such independent units formed in the parental house enjoy the benefits of a joint family household at times of need and also on festive occasions. Nandita said :

> "There is no other suitable accommodation for me than my father's part house. Five months back, I had an appendicitis operation and I was in the hospital for twelve days. I could leave my little children in my brother's family. I am really grateful to my brother's wife for taking care of them. Moreover, she had to look after me till my recovery". She further informed : "We observe festive occasions like *bihu*, birthdays of our children, religious performances, etc., as one family. On the night of *uruka*[15], we organise the feast together and prepare the *pithas*, with my brother's wife to celebrate the *bihu*".

The women living with their dependent children in rented house and quarters do not generally have the opportunity of getting help from their familial kin in the same manner.

The emotionalities between a woman and her children are very strong in the matri-centric families. Bakul, a college teacher, has three children — one son and two daughters. Narrating the relationship with her children, she said:

> "In the evening I have to remain busy with my children by taking them to their swimming class, music class or tuition. In the morning also I have to escort them to their school after arranging their dress and tiffin. I have little time for myself." Bakul is a divorcee.

Just five divorcees are living on their own with their children in dependent establishments. The childless divorcees of poor economic background are concentrated in different hostels and they thus do not create any family-like arrangement.

Only three unmarried women in the sample are members of nuclear family consisting of their parents and siblings. Mamata, an

---

[15]Uruka : The eve of *Magh bihu*.

unmarried teacher, lives with her father. After her mother's death, Mamata is staying alone with her old father. As she has no brother in her family, after the marriage of all her younger sisters, it is she who has to look after her father. She had to look after her mother also till her death. Regarding her father, Mamata said :

> "I cannot leave alone my old father except during the working hours. I do not ever go to cinema or theatre in the evening. Besides my personal work, I have to attend to various tasks for my father, e.g., work at bank, payments of land revenue, municipal tax and so on".

The bonds between an unmarried woman and her parents are thus found to be strong in this type of living arrangements in denuded nuclear families.

In the present study, the joint family for a single woman consists of her father, mother, unmarried siblings, married brothers, brothers' wives and brothers' children. This is in addition to any children she might have of her own. The majority of the single women found in the joint family-centred households are unmarried. The single women of other categories do not prefer to stay in a joint establishment. This is because of their limited income making it difficult for them to contribute adequately to the expenses of a joint household. At the same time, they do not want to be a burden on other members of the family and they also wish to be independent in terms of living arrangement. For reasons of security and protection, the unmarried women on the other hand do not usually think of leaving their parental family. Inclusive of such unmarried women 21.8 per cent of the single women live in joint family-centred households. Very few widows and divorcees are found living in joint family arrangement. They are mostly those who have returned to live in parental households. In a joint establishment, a woman is dependent on the male members of the family in many respects. An unmarried woman, though economically independent, consults her father or brother before taking any decision concerning her life.

In addition to living as part of the parental family, a few (8.2 per cent) of the women in the sample live with married brothers or unmarried siblings in extended family centred households.

> Senehi, a 28-year old widow with four children has kept a younger brother and a sister (both unmarried) with

her. As she has her own house, accommodation is not a problem. Senehi is earning Rs. 600.00 per month from her job as a record-arranger in a government office. In addition, she has some income from her cultivable land. Her unemployed brother helps her in cultivation while the unmarried sister, who stopped her studies in class ten, helps her with domestic chores.

The attitude of dependence is clearly perceptible among the single women in Assamese society. Discussions with the women reveal this attitude. They like to depend on their near kin if they have willing kin to help and assist them.

Table 27 shows that 41.0 per cent of the women in the sample live in setting which cannot be called family. These women are living on their own in different establishments for one or another reason : lack of support from familial kin, poverty or the desire to be independent.

The educated women, who have reasonable incomes, prefer to live on their own. Some of them opined that it is difficult to adjust in a family when they have their own career and job. They are mostly unmarried women residing in hostels and rented houses.

Some single women, however, would like to live in family establishments but cannot afford to do so because of their meagre incomes. Some widows and divorcees are unable to keep their children with them because of the limited accommodation they have in the city and their poor salaries.

Patterns of kin relationship

Kinship ties beyond the confines of the family are essential to the understanding of social organization. As Herskovits says : "Social organization is customarily studied in terms of two broad classes of institutions — those that grow out of kinship, and those that result from the free association of individuals. Kinship structures include the family and its extension into broader relationship groupings such as the clan" (1958:167). An attempt is made first to study kinship ties of the single women in relation to their families and also the nature of ties with other kin. Secondly, an attempt is also made to discuss the nature of social relations with non-kin individuals. There are social forces which lead to relationships with the non-kinsfolk (Kuppuswamy 1977:401). The organizing principles of kinship, therefore, is extended to persons outside the home which include friends and neighbours.

The analysis of cases reveals that the pattern of kinship bond among the single women is variable. Spread of education, occupational diversification, legislation regarding ownership and inheritance of land and other property and marriage and divorce, along with urban-industrial developments have influenced the sphere of kinship and individual's dependence on it.

As much as 51 per cent of the single women in the sample maintain fairly strong kinship ties with their kinfolk. These ties indicate thc dependent status of the women on kinship for support and assistance. Even when a woman has an independent source of livelihood she is dependent on her kin in various ways. The majority of these women are widows and unmarried, residing in their parental homes. The parental family is the place where a single woman gets the opportunity to come in contact with the relatives on both the father's and the mother's sides besides her siblings.

Discussing the nature of inter-personal ties in kinship, Dipika, a widow, said :

> "Besides the help I receive from the members of my parental family, my paternal and maternal uncles are also very much sympathetic and helpful towards me. My children sometimes go to spend their vacations with them. But I have no time to visit them except on special occasions". Regarding the paucity of time being a working woman, she further added : "Last December, I had to attend the wedding of my maternal uncle's daughter at Nagaon. But I could stay there only for the wedding night as I had no leave to extend my stay".
>
> Ranjana, another widow and a teacher also mentioned the same difficulties of not getting enough time to visit her kin. She said : ".... But I try to visit my mother-in-law's place in Sibsagar during *bihu* holidays. Though I am living with my parents, I like to meet my husband's family along with my son". Minakhsi thus tries to maintain her ties with her affinal kin.

The widows continuing to live in their own house after the

demise of their husbands, have the opportunity to maintain llinks with their affinal kin much more than the others.

> Senehi's husband dies after nine years of her marriage. She has maintained effective ties with her husband's brothers. She informed : "My husband's elder brother comes to see my children every Sunday. Occasionally on holidays he takes them to his house for the whole day. It is not very far from my house and therefore I also visit them occasionally". Regarding help and co-operation from affinal kin, she further said :" Both the elder and the younger brothers of my husband come to my help when occasion so requires. They always take interest in my children's education. I also like to discuss everything with them". On enquiry, Senehi informed that she has a plot of agricultural land measuring five bighas. As she said, her unmarried younger brother is looking after her land and cultivation by staying with her. Thus she is getting help and co-operation from both her affinal and consanguineal kin.

But divorce or separation raises certain complications in the pattern of kinship relationship of a single woman. Divorce usually creates difficulties for a woman to maintain effective and harmonious ties with her husband's family. Her kinship ties tend to be re-canalized towards her parental family. The women, like Pranati, Rumi, Gita, who have returned to the parental family following divorce, receive help and co-operation from parents and siblings.

> Pragati, an educated divorcee aged 45, said :"In my parental family, besides the other members, my father's elder sister is also very much sympathetic to me. She loves me like her own daughter. She is an unmarried retired school teacher as well as a social worker. As she has nobody to inherit her property, she has gifted her residential house to me by making a will". Pragati said that she has no effective ties with the members of her divorced husband's family. Niru, another educated divorcee, reported that she always tries to avoid her affines when she meet them.

The unmarried sigle women are naturally confined to the network of kinship through the parents. The women who have opted for a single life to support their respective families, expect recognition and understanding from the members of their familial kin. Chaya, Renuka and Mayatara are loved and respected by their brothers and sisters for whose welfare they chose to remain single. But Uma is not at all satisfied with her married younger brother. She said with some sadness :

> "I have more or less sacrificed my own life to support my family. I could not think of marrying because I had to support my brother's education. But at the age of 48 I am now repenting. After getting married, he only thinks of his wife and children".

While support from kinsfolk is coveted by single women of all the three categories, the study reveals that 32 per cent of the women have much to complain and lament on this aspect of traditional Assamese social organization. Besides, many professional and working women find it difficult to maintain effective ties with their kinsfolk. Purnima and Bandana, both doctors, are busy in their work. Kalyani, a lawyer, is busy in her legal practice. On being asked, Kalyani reported that she does not get time even to write a letter to her younger sister who lives in upper Assam.

Poor economic condition is another important factor which weakens kinship bonds. A poor father or a brother having his wife and children to support is not able to take the responsibility of a single woman who has the need for kin support.

> Nirala, hailing from a village of Kamrup, narrated the extreme poverty of her deceased husband's family in the following manner : "They are very poor cultivators and not in a position to help me. My parents too are very poor. So instead of going back to my parents, I have come to the city in search of livelihood".

There are many such instances in the sample. Lack of support from kinsfolk compels many of these women to seek shelter in the homes for destitutes.

Friends and neighbours

The patterns of behaviour appropriate to kin are sometimes extended to cover friends and neighbours. Because of the need for adjustment in the changing social milieu after becoming single, woman often gets involved in kinship like ties with friends and neighbours. In the case of a widow or divorcee, the friend circle of her husband often discontinues effective ties with her after the death of the husband or the dissolution of marriage. New bonds of friendship often emerge replacing the old ties.

> Sumitra, a 31-year old widow, hails from a village of Goalpara district. Her husband was an Inspector in the Health department who died of cancer. After his death, she was informed by one of her husband's friends regarding the post of a matron in a hostel for working women. Accordingly, she tried for the post with the help of her husband's friend and got the job. She left her husband's family in the village to join the post. Recalling about links with her husband's friend, Sumitra said : "After being employed, I have lost contact with the villagers as well as this and other friends of my husband".

> Taramai, another widow, whose husband was a fitter, is appointed as a peon in Railway department. Her husband was suffering from paralysis for about eight years till his death. Taramai had to face great financial hardship when her husband was in hospital. She had to maintain her family of five children. She sold some of her movable properties like ornaments, utensils, bicycle of her husband to meet her needs. She was also helped by her husband's friends and colleagues during those difficult days. Expressing her gratitude, Taramai said : "My husband's friends helped me a lot at the time of his death and performance of *Sradlha*. Only with their help I could get this job in my husband's office". But Taramai said that effective contacts with her husband's friends did not continue for long.

The study reveals that a gradual change comes over former ties of friendship with the passage of time due to change of residence, demands of job and so on. In addition, many single women also develop an attitude of avoiding social contacts with earlier friends and acquaintances. Her social world becomes somewhat narrower than before. However, in the course of her adjustment in the role of a single woman, she usually develops friendship with a new but limited circle of individuals. They are mainly her colleagues at the place of work, usually other women workers and especially with other single women. With other single women it is possible to establish empathy easily and she can discuss freely with them about her personal problems and difficulties. As a respondent said, a married woman does not realise the problems of a single woman and hence deep friendship between a married woman and a single woman seldom develops.

> Renuka, a spinster and a permanent resident of the city said : "Most of the women of my age are now wives and mothers. They have husbands, children and families to talk about; but I have to keep quiet when I meet them and the discussions veer round such a topic".

The relationship of a single woman with her neighbours is also very much limited. She usually does not find much leisure to visit neighbours for a friendly chat. But she tries to maintain her relationship with them by visiting on some particular occasions like illness, accident or death in a neighbouring family and in other unavoidable situations. Though the single women are not able to keep close informal contacts with their neighbours, they are also dependent on their neighbours to some extent.

> Bani, an unmarried teacher lives alone in rented accommodation near her school. When enquired about her relations with the neighbouring families, she said : "Though I am living alone, my next-door neighbours readily come to my help at times of need. Last month I had high fever for about three days. My neighbour Mrs. Saikia helped me a lot by sending her son for a doctor and by bringing medicine besides looking after me in many ways".

It appears that visiting as a form of social intercourse is not a common practice with single women. Besides lack of time and opportunity, there is a sense of uneasiness felt by many of them because of their single status. After being labelled as 'inauspicious' for the death of her husband, it is natural for a widow to avoid all the auspicious rites and ceremonies. Hesitation comes to her mind when a divorcee knows that she may be asked by the inquisitive about her husband in a social gethering. The same is the case with an unmarried woman who is afraid of facing question regarding her single status.

Only 14.5 per cent of the women in the sample are found to be involved in extensive social visits and informal interactions.

They are well educated women belonging to higher income group. Some of them have high status in society.

Religious activities

The Assamese Hindu womenfolk have certain traditionally defined roles and responsibilities in the sphere of religion. The cleaning of the altar, lighting of the lamp in the evening at the *gosai-ghar* and daily prayer after the bath in the morning are some of the tasks which are typically feminine. Unlike the typical housewife, most of the single women are, however, busy in earning their livelihood and have often the added responsibilities of bringing up children. They have to attend to work outside the house, perform household chores, do the shopping, pay taxes and electricity bill, look after the children and help them in their studies and so on. Many of them, therefore, cannot devote themselves to daily religious activities for a long time. In the month of Bhadra (August-September) the Assamese Hindu women usually attend the prayer meet at *namghars* every afternoon. But a single woman, who is also a working woman, does not usually get the time to attend such daily prayers. She devotes less on daily rituals. Most of them, however, have some sort of an altar for offering prayers at horne adorned with images or pictures of their favourite deities like Goddess Lakshmi or Lord Krishna. They offer their morning and evening prayers at such shrines in their homes. The widows are as a rule more involved in daily prayers and religious activities.

The religious life of a widow is influenced to some extent by her caste. A Brahmin or a high caste widow is more orthodox and follows customs and usages more rigorously than others. She has also to follow certain restrictions in diet. Her austere diet does not generally contain meat, fish, egg, lentil, onion, etc. She has to observe fasts on some particular days of the lunar calendar e.g., *amabashya, purnima, ekadashi* and *ambubashi*[16]. But due to the changed social circumstances of a single woman, there are deviations from these traditional norms and observances.

---

[16] *amabashya* : the day of the conjunction of the sun and moon;
purnima : the day of the full moon;
ekadashi : the eleventh day of the lunar half of the moon;
ambubashi : four days in the month of Assarh (June-July) when the earth is supposed to be unclean.

Recalling her village life in a rural area of lower Assam, Sashi, a childless Brahmin widow of 46 years, said :

> "I was a complete vegetarian in my village. I even did not take *masur dal* (lentil) and onion. But now in my hostel, it is difficult to observe these restrictions. I have to adjust to my situation. I now eat *masur dal* and onion in the hostel, but not fish, meat or egg. As I have no problem in observing fast, I follow it on the *ekadashi* tithi".
>
> Kuntala, another Brahmin widow who lives independently in her allotted quarters reported : "Though I have to prepare fish, meat and egg for my children, I do not myself consume these items forbidden for a widow. For one year after my husband's death, I did not even take *masur dal* and onion. But being a working woman it is difficult for me to follow all the restrictions of widowhood". She further informed that in the year following her husband's death, she observed the restrictions on food during the three days of *ambubashi.* Recalling her experience she said :
>
> "I had to preserve drinking water, fruits and other edibles for the period. Partaking of cooked food was not allowed during the *ambubashi* period and I took only *kecha* (uncooked) food. Touching earth was also prohibited. But I could not follow all the restrictions because of my little children. My widowed mother is still observing these special restrictions".

For a working woman it is difficult to take leave from duty for three days to observe the *ambubashi.* It is therefore seen that this old practice is not followed by the single women in the contemporary Assamese Hindu society. But fasting and visiting temples and *namghars* are the part of their religious life. Not only the Brahmins, the elderly widows of other castes also observe many religious customs and norms.

Subhasini, a 57-year old Kayastha widow, visits the nearby temple whenever she gets the time. She said :

> "Ugratara temple is near my house. On my way to school I pass by the side of the temple and bow down my head from the road. It is a regular practice with me". She is a pure vegetarian and fasts on *ekadashi tithi.*

> Dipika, 42, a Kayastha widow is a devotee of Satya Sai Baba. The walls of her room are adorned with pictures of Sai Baba.
>
> Dipti, another Kayastha widow of 39, visits Sukreswar temple regularly every Monday morning to offer her prayers. She is a childless widow residing with her widowed mother.

The childless young widows do not tend to observe the death anniversary of their husbands in any special way. Mallika, Minakhsi, Bijaya, Kalyani are such examples. When asked about the date of her husband's death, Kalyani, a practising lawyer, said:

> "I have forgotten the exact date of his death. Perhaps it was in the last week of January. Why should I remember such a painful day? I do not like to observe his death anniversary and the date is therefore not so important to me. I have the respect and regard for the departed soul in the corner of my heart". She lost her husband only after six months of her marriage (*see* pp. 111-12).

Some widows whose children are still very young observe the death annivesaries of their husbands by performing *namkirttan* in their homes or by offering *pinda*[17] in the temple of Aswaklanta by the side of the river Brahmaputra.

> Senehi, a young widow of 28, said : "My eldest son is only 9 years old. I therefore perform the *sraddha* caremony of my deceased husbnd by myself at the temple of Aswaklanta and offer *pinda* with the help of the temple priest".

Among the single women of lower income group, it is found that due to poor economic condition and social constraints, they are not vey much concerned with the observance of *sraddha* of their deceased husbands.

> Sumitra, a matron of a working girls' hostel does not observe the death anniversary of her deceased husband. She is a Brahmin widow. She said "where is the money to perfom *sraddha*? I earn Rs. 175.00 a month from which I

---

[17] *pinda* : an oblation of cake, prepared by rice mixed with milk, sugar, honey, etc., offered to the manes of a deceased person.

> have to pay Rs. 120.00 for food to the hostel authority". Because of economic reasons and her hostel life, it is not at all possible to observe such rites.

A widow generally does not participate in ceremonies regarded auspicious by society. For example, she keeps herself away from taking active part in certain wedding rites of even close relative.

In the context of *namghar*, it is seen that a widow takes an active part in the religious activities. Sweeping and cleaning the *namghar*, preparing the *prasad* (food offered to the deity), etc., are duties in which widows are actively involved in Assamese society. On the other hand, an unmarried woman is not permitted to do these works in a place of worship. An unmarried woman is called *abiyoi* in Assamese language which indicates an impure status of a woman in the Assamese society (Barua 1978:97). An *abiyoi* is not allowed to cook food in the orthodox families of Assam.

> Jaya, Kayastha by caste and an unmarried school teacher, said : "If my grandmother comes from our village home, my widowed mother cooks food for her; she does not take any food cooked by me". Jaya is also not allowed to take any active part in religious activities of the family, as she informed.
>
> Padmini, a 37-year old unmarried lawyer, hailing from Barpeta, has narrated the position of unmarried women in religious activity and said : "We are not permitted to perform any religious tasks in a temple or a *namghar*, not even allowed to kindle the earthen lamp".
>
> Bani, an unmarried school teacher, informed that at her brother's wedding she and her widowed mother kept away from certain rituals. "These feminine rites were attended to by my married sister", Bani said. She also informed that though her married younger sister is a divoree, she is not debarred unlike a widow or an *abiyoi*. There are no specific restrictions or observances for a divorcee or a separated woman in the religious sphere.

Leisure and recreation

In the traditional rural Assamese society, women's leisure time activities are usually confined to visiting neighbours and gossiping with friends and spending time on the household loom. In the urban context, weaving as a domestic activity is practically non-existent. Informal social visits to relatives, friends and neighbours as well as shopping are common leisure time activities of urban Assamese women. The single women in the sample, however, have very little leisure time to devote to these recreational activities.

> Durpati, a polythene bag-maker and widowed mother of four children, said : "where do we get the time or the money to go out for fun? I leave the house at nine in the morning and get back in the evening. Sundays are always occupied with my household work. But for the pleasure of my children, sometimes I go with them to the cinema, if any Assamese film is shown".

The divorcees and unmarried women consider cinema as their favourite entertainment. Many educated widows are interested in reading light story books and novels as a leisure time activity. Radio is also a source of entertainment for the single women. Damayanti, an *ayah* of a middle English school, informed:

> "I like to listen to the radio even while cooking. During my leisure time, sometimes, I like to be engaged in weaving while listening to the radio".

Television is nowadays becoming a new source of entertainment for the single women belonging to higher income group. Bandana, a doctor and Dipika, an executive officer, consider television as their favourite entertainment.

Gardening, cooking, knitting and embroidery are also leisure time activities for some.

A few women in the sample have a musical bent of mind and are themselves singers or players of musical instruments.

> Purnima, a 39-year old widowed medical practitioner, often plays violin in the evenings after her duty hours. Mamata, a 44 years old unmarried educated woman likes to play *sitar*. She has also obtained a *Bisharad* degree in *sitar* performance. Bani another 49-year old unmarried woman is fond of singing and listening to *bhajan*. She attends *bhajan* performances every Tuesday, organized at different homes in her locality. She is a Montessory School teacher and devotee of Satya Sai Baba.

A number of women have the habit of reading books. The reading habits of these women are directly related to their educational level and to some extent to their socio-economic status. Subhasini studied up to matric level after her husband's death and was appointed as a teacher in a lower primary school. She said :

> "I like to read particularly travel story. These are very interesting but religious books also give me pleasure". Basanti, Kuntala, Maikan and Sarumai, all women with modest education are interested in reading religious books, e.g., Assamese versions of the *Ramayana, Mahabharata* and *Gita*.

Some women are involved in welfare-oriented and cultural organizations. Senehi, a widow, is an active member of a *Sisu Kalyan Samiti*, a children's welfare organization located in her area. She said :

> "I am always interested in attending meetings or any other programme of the *samiti*. But it depends on my having time and the opportunity". Senehi is employed in an office as a record-arranger. Kamala, separated woman, is a superintendent of a girls' hostel. She is a member of a social welfare organization. Nilima, an unmarried high school teacher, is a honorary secretary of a women's organization in the city.

The very poor single women are completely pre-occupied in eking out a living and the prospect of recreational activities hardly arise in their case.

Dress and ornaments

The majority of the single women mention the Assamese *mekhela-chadar* as the dress of their choice. But a *pat* or *muga mekhela* is costly to afford for daily use, especially at work. A cotton *mekhela* is not considered elegant and comfortable. Therefore many prefer saree for daily use. Moreover, it has become a trend in Assamese society to wear saree instead of the traditional Assamese dress as a sort of adjustment to modern life. But a woman generally likes to wear the Assamese dress on festive and ceremonial occasions. e.g., *bihu* and wedding. On religious occasions also it is customary to wear the traditional Assamese dress. This is of course the general pattern among Assamese womenfolk as a whole. Most of the women hailing from the rural areas, wear cotton *mekhela* and *chadar* woven in hand looms.

A widow is generally dressed in white and not in coloured fabrics. After her husband's death, she is to wear white *mekhela* and *chadar* and this dress pattern is supposed to be followed during her widowhood. She is also not allowed to wear any ornaments. The ornaments and the vermillion mark of her forehead are removed by some of her nearest kin following the death of her husband. This custom still prevails in Assamese society.

> Sashi, a childless Brahmin widow of 46 years, does not approve of widows in coloured dress. "I have been wearing white dress and have shunned ornaments since 1948. I do not want to break the prevailing norms of our society", she said. Kuntala, 37, a Brahmin widow with two children is also of the same opinion. Both of them hail from rural areas of lower Assam and have limited education.

Besides the Brahmin, the widows of other castes hailing from the rural areas are still reluctant to wear ornaments and coloured fabrics. But some educated widows hailing from urban areas wear coloured dress as well as ornaments and also put on *bindi* on the forehead. In dress and ornaments they cannot be distinguished from other women. Nandita, Mallika, Dipika, Ranjana — they are all the natives of Guwahati. They do not go about wearing widow's attire. As for other single women who are not widows, one cannot find any special feature in dress and ornaments, except perhaps that many of them tend to be somewhat austerely dressed even when they can afford to dress expensively.

Attitude towards marriage and remarriage

Marriage is regarded as necessary social stage in the life of a person by most of the single women in the sample. The attitudes of the respondents are shown in Table 28.

Table 28 shows a high percentage (63.6) of single women with favourable attitude towards marriage and remarriage. Many of these respondents are women who have never entered into matrimony. The women who have not yet married due to various compelling circumstances often harbour the hope of getting married.

Table 28
Attitude of the respondents towards marriage and remarriage

Attitudes	Widow	Divorcee	Unmarried	Total	
				Number	Per cent
Favourable	28	11	31	70	63.6
Unfavourable	12	19	9	40	36.4
.	40	30	40	110	100.0

The women who never married in order to support their families or for other reasons often repent their action. The necessity of company, social security, protection and status in society is now felt by them. During the period of this study, instances were found of respondents getting married at a late age. Amiya got married at the age of 44 and Padmini at 37. Anju and Ila were still hoping to get married at the age of 34. Some spinsters have clear opinions against marriage because of their very special circumstances in life, e.g., dedication to social work and pursuit of career.

Next to unmarrieds, the widowed women show a favourable attitude to marry again. Owing to the efforts of Isvarachandra Vidyasagara remarriage of a widow had become possible under the Hindu Widow Remarriage Act of 1856. But even now, more than a hundred years after this enactment, remarriage of a widow is not regarded as normal by most of the people in the contemporary Assamese Hindu society. In some of the rural areas of Kamrup and Goalpara districts, among certain peasant castes, a young widow is often taken in as a wife although the wedding rites are somewhat simplified. But it can be considered as a deviation from the norm of the existing society. The widow remarriage is a new phenomenon in the Assamese Hindu society. Only 7.5 per cent of the widowed respondents are found to be remarried. Though the percentage of widow remarriage is very small, it seems that most of the respondents feel remarriage should become more widespread. The reasons behind favourable attitude, emerging from interviews with the women in the sample, are : social security and protection of the woman; economic help and co-operation which a husband alone can provide to regain the status of a married woman; to enjoy motherhood and raise children (in case of childless widow) : to get the joys and satisfaction of conjugal life; and, to have company in life.

Most parents do not like to see their young daughters in the status of a widow. If not very conserative, they try for her remarriage during their life time to ensure her security and happiness. For the necessity of social security and protection of a young widow, the question of caste affiliation and marital status of the groom are generally not important factors in remarriage. The groom may be a divorcee or a widower.

> Mallika offers an example of one who had to accept the decision of her father to marry again. She is a Kayastha by caste. Her father is a retired top official occupying a high status in society. He did not like to see his only daughter leading the life of a widow. All her brothers had their own respective families to maintain and she was therefore dependent on her retired father. The father discussed the importance of remarriage with his widowed daughter and with her consent arranged her marriage with a man working as a government officer. The man was a divorcee and belonged to the Kaibartta caste — a caste lower in the hierarchy than her own. The remarriage was solemnized in a very simple way by registration in the court in 1984. In most of the cases of remarriage it is found that widowers come forward to marry a widowed woman.
>
> Bijaya, a childless widow of the Kayastha caste, was asked about the prospect of her remarriage. With a favourable attitude to marry a widower, she informed : "I have received three proposals for remarriage after the death of my husband. One of these is from a widower with a son. He is an employee in my same office where I work and is of the same caste as my own. I have not yet refused the proposal. But I have also received another proposal from one of my friends belonging to my same village and same caste. We know each other from our childhood". After about six months of the interview, Bijaya married the man hailing from her village by registration in the court.
>
> Ranjana, a school teacher, has a son studying in class VII. She is a Kayastha by caste and is the only daughter of her parents. After he husband's death, she was helped in many ways by one of her husband's friends. He was an unmarried engineer and he proposed to marry her. But she could not acccept the proposal because of her child. She

thought that there might be problems for her son if she married again. Her parents came forward to take the responsibilities of bringing up her son and on their pressure she agreed to marry again. Though Ranjana is Kayastha by caste, she has married a man belonging to the Ahom community. The latter did not hasitate to marry a widow having a grown up son. This was possible only because of the mutual understanding between the two.

Instances of remarriage of widows having more than one child are also found. Lakhmi, Kaibartta by caste, is a peon with two children aged about 7 and 4 years, respectively. Regarding her remarriage, she informed; "It was arranged by one of my colleagues, who is also a widow, much older to me. The person is her younger brother and was a widower with a three-year old son. He is also a peon belonging to the Kaibartta caste. After being informed about the person, I decided to marry him for the welfare of my two children and also to have a secure life".

Such remarriages are usually peformed by registration and not celebrated as regular weddings in Assamese society.

Regarding her new married life and reactions from her social group, Lakhmi said : " Though both of us belong to the same caste, I had to face various criticisms from some of my neighbours and kin. The members of my deceased husband's family did not like it at all. They thought that after remarriage, there would be no relation between them and my former husband's family, who also live in the city. Thus I try to keep relations with them". She was further proudly admitted:"My second husband is a very considerate man and we have a good understanding. Both of us are now enjoying peace and harmony with all our children. Now I feel secure in society".

On the other hand, some respondents show unfavourable attitude towards remarriage of a widow and cite various reasons : e.g., the prospect of such a marriage not working since it is difficult to love and adjust with another man in life; absence of guarantee for survival of a second marriage; fear of stress in the relationship between the children and the step mother/father; and, absence of encouragement to remarriage in the traditional and conservative Assamese society.

Among the divorced or separated women in the sample only 11 respondents have a favourable attitude towards remarriage. Out of 30 interviewed women, 19 have unfavourable attitude to marry again. The cause behind such unfavourable attitude is that since divorce is a legal process, women are not free to marry again without going to the court. Only through a legal process a separated husband and wife can change their obligations and privileges towards one another and restores the freedom to remarry. The present study shows that only in the higher socio-economic stratum marriage of a divorced woman has come to be somewhat accepted.

Thus Table 28 shows, 36.4 per cent of the single women in the samaple have unfavourable attitudes to marriage and remarriage. Without entering into matrimony, some of these women try to make their career in various fields. Instead of getting remarried, some of them dedicate their lives to be career women to compensate the loss of husband.

But career-making attitude is not seen among the women of lower and middle economic strata. They are not able to think of career beyond their day-to-day problems.

A single woman is deprived of a proper family environment in her day-to-day life. The biological, emotional and sccio-cultural urges remain significantly unfulfilled in the life of a single woman. For whatever reasons a woman has to remain single, some of the socio-economic factors of her life have physical manifestations causing certain stress-induced ailments. As a respondent, herself a medical practitioner, remarked breast cancer or some gynaecological disorders are observed little higher in case of single women, especially in case of unmarried, than that of other female population. Hysteria, phobia of various kinds, anxiety-neurosis are some of the mental conditions which, according to her, more common in single women.

11

SINGLE WOMEN AND LEGAL PROVISIONS

In India, legislations relating to women's rights and their status in society have so far made no appreciable impact on their life. Discussing the difficulties faced by women, particularly Hindu women, Minattur (1980:166) notes : "During the last two decades a number of laws were adopted with a view to ensuring equality of status and opportunity for women. But it appears that in practice this equally eludes the Indian woman's grasp". Another author also expresses similar views on the legal aspects of the status of Indian women. In an assesment she states the position of women in the following words : "Legislation enacted during the last two decades is out of reach for most women because, by and large, they have neither the mental awareness nor the financial resources to take advantage of these beneficent provisions" (Pappu 1975:115).

Like other parts of the country, in Assam too the women are not getting adequate opportunity to exercise their legal rights and freedom in society. They are socially and economically not capable of reaping the benefits of law. This will be evident when we examine the provisions of some important legislations in relation to the position of single women in Assamese society in the spheres of marriage, maintenance and succession.

Marriage

Since family is regarded as the basic unit of social structure, one of the major fields where there has been interaction between law and social thinking is matrimonial law. Because marriage and family are complementary institutions, we shall at first discuss the important provisions of certain legislation relating to marriage.

i. *Child marriage :*

The prevalence of child marriage in India, leading often to early widowhood, was one of the major concerns of the social reformers in the early part of this century. With a view to preventing child marriage, the Child Marriage Restraint Act was passed in 1929. Under the provisions of this Act, the minimum age of marriage was eighteen years for female and fourteen years for female. The age for female was raised to fifteen years in 1949. After the amendment of the said Act in 1978, the age of marriage has been raised to eighteen years for female and twenty one years for male (Current Indian Statutes 1978 : 3). According to this Act not only a man who marries a girl below the age of 18, but also the following classes of persons are also punishable for promoting child marriage: *(i)* parents or guardians who permit a child marriage or negligently fail to prevent such marriage and *(ii)* any person who performs, conducts or directs child marriage to be solemnized (the All India Reporter manual 1979:132). But these restrictions have yet to be very effective in the Assamese Hindu society. The present study shows that about 25.7 per cent of the widows and divorcees in the sample had to enter into matrimony before the age of fifteen. They fell into the single status at relatively early ages because of their marriage at tender age.

Marriage at an early age is a customary practice specially among the Brahmins in the Assamese society. As evident from the statements of the respondents of Brahmin caste, most of them were married just after the attainment of puberty. But in some of the orthodox families in rural areas, it has been found that a girl was married off by her parents even before she attained puberty.

> Sashi, a Brahmin widow was married at the age of twelve in 1948, before she attained puberty. She hails from a village of South Kamrup. She said, "I did not see any school during my childhood. Instead of giving education, my parents arranged my marriage at an early age". As she

> informed, her *santi-biya* took place six months after she attained her puberty. Her husband died only twenty days after her conjugal life began. Thus she became a widow at a very tender age.

Like early widowhood a woman married off at a tender age may become single rather early in life through divorce or separation.

> Bhanu, a separated woman, was given in marriage in 1969 at the tender age of nine. She is the daughter of a devout Brahmin of a renowned *satra*, some 70 km away from Guwahati. Her husband also belonged to the same satra and he was only nineteen years old at the time of their marriage. She said : "Early marriage is a custom in our Brahmin families. Just after I passed the primary examination, my parents selected the boy for my marriage. I had no say in the matter and had to enter into matrimony accordingly". She further added, "But after marriage, I was in my parents' house till the attainment of puberty. After following the customary rule of *santi-biya,* I came to my husband's house to stay with him". Unfortunately as she has reported, Bhanu could live with her husband no longer than about three months. Soon after marriage, she came to know that her husband had an illicit relationship with a girl from a neighbouring village and he was planning to marry that girl very soon. Therefore, separation with her husband took place when she was below fifteen. Thus she came to acquire single status at a very early stage in life.

The practice of child marriage was common among the Brahmins and the high caste Hindus in the Assamese society in the earlier years. Nowadays, age at marriage has gone up even in the villages. But under certain socio-economic circumstances, early marriage still prevails in the rural areas of Assam, irrespetive of caste.

> Apati, a sparated woman of Kalita caste was married at the age of 14, just after attaining puberty, at a village in the district Kamrup. Her father died when she was only one year old. Her widowed mother maintained the family by working in other persons' agricultural fields. Being

helpless, the poor mother arranged her marriage soon after she attained puberty.

Assumption of responsibility of an unmarried daughter is a problem not only for a poor widow, but also for a poor father. In the rural areas of Assam, most of the people are poor peasants. Distressed by economic hardship, they often try to marry off their daughters in a humble manner as early as possible. Kunti, a widow of Kalita caste, is the eldest of her parents' eight children. Born in a poor peasant family, she did not attend any school. She was taught all the household work by her mother. After attaining puberty at the age of thirteen, she was given away in marriage by her parents.

Among adverse socio-economic circumstances, orphanage, besides poverty, is also another factor of child marriage. It is the customary duty of her kin to take the responsibility of such an orphan. So her marriage is an obligatory duty of her near kin. Naturally they try to discharge this responsibility at the earliest opportunity.

> Basanti, a widow of Kaibartta caste, was married at the age of thirteen. She was a posthumous child of her widowed mother. Her mother also died when she was only two. She was then brought up by her mother's brother. After she attained puberty, she was given away in marriage by her maternal uncle in order to lessen his burden. Likewise, Taramai's parents died of cholera when she was only one year old (*see* pp. 216-17). She was brought up by her father's brother Taramai narrated with some sorrow: "Instead of going to school with my uncle's daughter, I had to help my aunt in her household work. My uncle was a poor peasant. So I was a burden to him. Just after attaining puberty, I was given away in marriage at the age of twelve".

These are some of the instances of the practice of child marriage found in the rural areas of Assam even after the enactment of the Child Marriage Restraint Act, as amended in 1978 or Hindu Marriage Act of 1955. From the above cases, it can be inferred that the said Acts have been less effective in practice due chiefly to (a) predominance of the customary laws; (b) ignorance of the provisions of these laws and (c) adverse socio-economic circumstances.

ii. *Remarriage :*

As revealed in the study, widowhood at a tender age arises out of the practice of child marriage. Most such widows in the sample have to lead the traditional pattern of widow's life from an early age. Though the Hindu Widow's Remarriage Act was enacted as early as 1856. The practice never became widely prevalent. It is important to note that only 7.5 per cent of the women covered in the sample of widows remarried during the course of field-work.

Remarriage of a divorced woman is still regarded as a deviation from norm. Only two educated respondents, out of the 30 divorcees in the sample, entered into matrimony again after being divorced by obtaining decrees from the court.

Assamese women in general are shy about going to the court for any relief under the provisions of the Acts, e.g., the Hindu Marriage Act which provides for divorce and prohibits bigamy. Manimala does not like to move the court to get a decree of divorce, though she is a highly educated woman. She said :

> "Going to the court is always an ugly business. It is no fun. Even when a woman files a petition for assertion of her rights, she has got to stand up in front of strangers in the court and describe how she was beaten, abused, exploited by her husband, and so on. Do you think it is easy?"

Moreover, the problem is partly financial. It is an expensive proposition for most women to move the court. The respondents who have attained decrees of divorce are either daughters of rich parents or belong to the higher income group.

It is revealed by the study that the percentage of divorced women who have been benefited by the legal relief is very low, being only 23.3. The others who are classified as 'separated women' are those whose marriages are broken because of lack of harmony without going to any court for legal relief. The percentage of such women is 76.6. A poor woman who is at the same time uneducated has neither the knowledge nor the means to move the court to obtain a decree of divorce under the provisions of the Hindu Marriage Act.

While bigamy has been made an offence under the provisions

of the Hindu Marriage Act, bigamous marriage is still prevalent in society. Table 20 (*see* p. 128) shows that 25 per cent of the separated women had broken marriages because of bigamous marriage of their husbands. Among them, only two respondents were able to move the court to file a suit against their respective husbands. They are urban and educated, aware of the provisions of law. Others are from rural areas belonging to very poor families.

Maintenance

Marriage confers on a husband the legal obligation to maintain his wife, provided she is chaste and unable to maintain herself. Wives, who are deserted, abandoned or neglected can claim maintenance from their husbands. The Hindu Adoption and Maintenance Act, 1956 [section 18 (2)] also provides that a Hindu wife shall be entitled to live separately from her husband without forfeiting her claim to maintenance (Desai 1986:1115). But getting alimony from the divorced husband by a woman and her dependent children is not easy. At times the husband is not solvent enough to make regular payments. At other times he wants to escape the responsibility.

The present study shows that only four among the divorced women are getting maintenance from their former husbands. These former husbands have adequate income to pay the alimony.

Two other respondents, are trying to get maintenance by filing suits in the court. Others are unable to move the court for lack of money, know-how, and help and also out of a sense of embarrassment.

Succession

Though there is legal provision under the Hindu Succession Act, 1956 (section 8), for a widow to succeed to the share of her husband's property (Desai 1986 : 940), it is still found to be ineffective in practice in the Assamese Hindu society. It is found that only 25 per cent of the widows could succeed to the shares of their deceased husbands' familial agricultural land. They have accepted whatever shares are given to them without taking any help of law. But the remaining 75 per cent of the widows in the sample have not got any benefit out of the relevant legal provisions. Some of these widows are very poor and their husbands left no land to be inherited by them. The others, who are childless widows do not like to claim any share out of their deceased husband's joint estate

The widows whose marriages were performed without any negotiation or the consent of the families on either side, often voluntarily gave up their shares of husbands' joint family property. Bandana, a doctor said:

> "As our marriage was not a negotiated marriage, I do not at all think of claiming any share of my deceased husband's property".
>
> Durpati, another widow also said in the same manner. She is Kaibartta by caste, but she was given in marriage by her father to a boy belonging to Jogi caste. The boy's family did not agree to this inter-caste. She has acquired the ownership right over her deceased husband's self-acquired land in Guwahati. She said : "I am not willing to claim any share of my husband's joint family land at Nagaon. Because of our inter-caste marriage, the members of my husband's family do not like to keep any links with me".
>
> Some of the widows hope to get shares of husbands' property. Taru Lata said that her husband owned agricultural land jointly with his parents and brothers in a rural area of Kamrup district. She said : "My husband was the second among the three brothers. His brothers are still cultivating the family land jointly. Therefore my share is not yet settled. But they sometimes give me a little paddy out of my share". In another case, Sarumai has been assured by her husband's elder brother that the share of her husband's joint agricultural land would be given to her. Sarumai's husband owned five bighas of agricultural land jointly with his elder brother at a village, about 32 km away from Guwahati. Both of them were cultivating the land together before her husband's death.

A woman in the Assamese society generally does not file a suit for recovering the property to which she is entitled. This is because of financial difficulties, lack of awareness and assistance from the kin. She has thus often to forego her share of husband's property.

> Subhasini's husband was the second among three brothers. She said : "Though my husband was a salaried employee in the Railway Department and lived in official quarters in Guwahati, he owned land jointly with his brothers in the village. But after his death the two other

brothers of my husband were unwilling to give any share of land to me. At the time of his death, my two sons were only four and two years, old, respectively. I was helpless and there was nobody in my family to help me in filing a suit claiming the property. I did not have enough money to engage a lawyer. So I had to give up my share".

Golapi's son was only nine months old at the time of her husband's death. She is deprived of her husband's property to which she is legally entitled. She complained: "My husband and his elder brother, jointly owned a house and a small plot of land at the eastern fringe of the city. But when I had to come to my parents' house after the bereavement, my brother-in-law occupied the whole house. Now he does not want to give me any share of that house and land. By convening a *mel*[18] in the *namghar* of the neighbourhood, I am now trying to recover the share for my only son. If I can somehow arrange the money, I am willing to file a suit in the court. But working as a *bai* (ayah) in a school, I get only Rs. 445.00 at the end of the month. Is it possible for me to move the court without money?"

Thus most of the women in the Assamese society do not appear to get any benefit from the enacted legislations.

Among the unmarried women, 20 per cent of the respondents have succeeded to their father's residential land or house. Ahalya and Mamata have no brothers and therefore being unmarried they have inherited their father's house and landed property. Their married sisters did not claim the property. Pranati and Padmini are the only issues of their parents and have inherited their parents' residential houses.

Enquiries revealed that in the Assamese society a father or a brother tries to provide a small plot of land or a part of a residential house, if available, to his unmarried dependent daughter or sister. It is usually considered an obligation for the father or brother and therefore an unmarried woman does not like to claim such property from them. In this, we can identify the role of familial kinship in the Assamese society. Even under the changed circumstances, a woman can hope to get some succour from her natal family. But the extent of such help and assistance are variable being dependent on the resources of the natal family and attitudes of the near kin.

---

[18] *mel* : a gathering of elders of a locality or village to decide on a dispute.

12

CONCLUDING OBSERVATIONS

The study of single women comprising widows, divorcees and ummarrieds in the contemporary Assamese Hindu society was undertaken with a view to finding out their emerging problems and status. A single woman is one who is required to look after herself and her dependents. The thesis has tried to unravel the quality of articulation and the pattern of adjustment of each category of single women in the modern Assamese society and also the distincitive aspects of their life and problems.

The study has been confined to single women living in the urban environs of Guwahati. The phenomenon of single women as an identifiable and somewhat discrete category has emerged in this city more markedly than any other town of Assam. This is because of the almost explosive urban growth of Guwahati in the last few decades which has created opportunities for education, employment and living outside the rigid and limited social environs of villages. Besides other migrants, many single women of diverse socio-economic background have found their way to this premier city of North-East India in the recent years. The urban setting of Guwahati has not merely provided a comparatively more flexible social environment for adjustment to the single women, but also opportunities to earn a living and thus giving them a measure of economic independence.

As a matter of fact, the concept of single women subsumes a degree of economic independence which accrues from their being involved in work outside the domestic arena. In other words, in order to maintain single status, a means of livelihood is necessary. Thus, as the study shows, most of the women in the sample are involved in salaried and wage jobs or in the professions. Earning a living, irrespective of the level of solvency, creates the very basis of single status for widows, divorcees and unmarried women.

It has been seen that in the sample of 110 women in the focal universe of 401, most (58.2 per cent) of the respondents have come to the city from different districts of Brahmaputra valley. According to Srinivas (1981:29), the migration to urban area enables women to make a relatively easy transition to new roles and responsibilities. In describing the position of women in India, he refers to the rural society and how female role and behaviour vary at different levels of caste hierarchy. Since Independence, opportunities for mobility have greatly increased for poor and low status Indians of rural society.

Among the migrants of the present study, 73.4 per cent of the single women belonged to peasant families of rural Assam. This clearly establishes the fact that progressive urbanization of Assam has an impact on rural women who otherwise would have been living as accretions and dependents in the households of near kin in their single status. Urban growth and development have thus led to the emergence of single women as a distinctive segment in the contemporary Assamese society.

As regards caste affiliation, it is found that the highest percentage (28.2 per cent) of single women in the sample belongs to the Kalita caste. It is followed by Brahmin (21 per cent), Kayastha (18.2 per cent) and Kaibartta (18.2 per cent). The Brahmins and the Kayasthas are reckoned in the Assamese caste hierarchy to have high social status, followed by the Kalitas who may be said to belong to middle rung of the social hierarchy. The Kaibarttas' traditional caste occupation is fishing and they are now recognised as one of the Scheduled Castes of Assam. Customary rules on widowhood, remarriage and remaining unmarried beyond a certain age are fairly rigid among the upper and middle castes and these caste conventions often induce women to remain single in life.

Modern education has fairly touched the women in the contemporary Assamese society. The sample covers single women of whom 80 per cent have had some education ranging from the primary to the post-graduate level. This high percentage is because of the selective nature of the sample concentrated in urban area. Education for these women has been like a bridge to employment. Literacy and education have paved the way for various jobs and occupations taken up by single women. Education and employment have thus created the potentials for social change.

The study has analyzed cases of single women to depict how they are pushed into single status. As regards widowhood, the highest number (29 out of 40 in the sample) became widow between the ages of 21 and 35. After the death of husband, the changed behaviour of husband's family members often makes it difficult for a woman to continue living with them. Added to this is the factor of economic condition. In a poor peasant household, the widow is regarded as a burden and her in-laws therefore refuse to maintain her. The joint family-centred household frequently breaks up following deaths. A widow often finds that her husband's death triggered such a break-up making her an unwelcome member in her in-laws' household. The changed circumstances after widowhood deprives her of shelter, safety and security; but at the same time these also induce her to look for alternative avenues of support, security and economic independence through employment of one sort or another.

Some women acquire single status through broken marriage, either by informal separation or formal divorce. Whether they are separated or divorced, their need to readjust in society is the same. The problems of striking an adjustment with the altered social circumstances are immense for such women. As one another notes: "After divorce, men face relatively fewer problems as compared with women. The Indian society is still partial in its attitude towards men. Men are economically independent. In most of the cases, they continue in their joint family; as a result, home management or even care of children poses no great problem [in the case of men]" (Pothen 1987:285). In the present study, out of 30 divorced women, 9 became single through broken marriages for various reasons at ages varying between 21 and 25 years. The cases indicate a very young age of the women at the time of becoming single through broken marriage.

The rising rate of literacy and education among women in the present day Assamese society has provided them with a measure of decision-making power. An unmarried woman often remains single on her own choice and decision. There are, of course, various compelling circumstances aiding her to decide to remain single. In the sample of 40 unmarried women, there are as many as 26 in the age range of 30-44 years.

Thus, many women in the contemporary Assamese Hindu society have come to be single women. In the context of Indian society as a whole, the number of widowed, divorced or separated and unmarried women, who can no longer expect to be fully supported by their familial kin is on the increase (*Report on the status of women in India* 1974:202). Loss of support from the bread-winners of the family caused by death or other reasons and the disintegration of joint families are the causes behind this situation. To quote D'Souza (1980:39) : "Widows often find themselves in tragic circumstances even if theoretically they should be held in high respect." Denoting the divorced and separted women as 'single mothers', he says that they do not have well-defined structural status. Institutional support or social acceptance may often be lacking (*abid.*).

In the present study, 42 per cent of the single women are in the 30-39 years age range. Many women became single at the peak of their lives. This enforces on them a new role to which they are required to adjust. The children of widows and divorcees are frequently so young that they are not in a position to help their mothers in playing the role of single parent.

In the emergent situation of single status, a woman feels the necessity of separate accommodation for herself and her children (when she has any). The cases have shown that four factors influence a single woman in making her living arrangement. These are, security, independence, economic viability and comfort. Security is a prime consideration since she has to live on her own or with very young children. To a married woman, the husband is a major prop for security, but to a single woman this opportunity is absent. The women have the following types of living arrangements : (i) own house, (ii) parental house, (iii) rented accommodation, (iv) allotted quarters and (v) hostel.

Very few women (17.3 per cent) are fortunate enough to have own house. Most of those who own house are widows. The widows have some advantage in this matter over the two other categories. In some cases the husband left behind the house or a half-finished house. Besides, some widows received each from the settlement of life insurance policies and provident fund of the husbands. Thus, fund was available to build a house. A divorced woman gets almost nothing from her husband and only those who have good jobs and high income are able to build their own houses. An unmarried woman, does not usually feel any need to construct her own house till her parents' death.

The number of single women living in the parental house is large (28.2 per cent). The parental house offers the best possible security to such single women. Where the parents are well-to-do, economic support is also ensured. This indicates that familial relationship still ensures help and support to single women in the changing Assamese society. In her study of divorced Hindu women relating mainly to urban society in Northern India, Mehta (1975:15) also points out that the parental house provided secure living arrangement for such women. She notes that the parental home gives them a feeling of security and respectablity. As the author further notes, "... were it not for the shelter given by their parental homes, they could not have taken the step of breaking up their marriage at the time they did" (*ibid.*). But even then the women covered in her study consider their position as imperfect in their parental home, as is the situation obtaining in the Assamese society. This happens especially when the authority of managing the house passes on to a sister-in-law (brother's wife). To quote Mehta again : "The feeling of not having any rights in their parental homes, even when the respondents were whole-heartedly received, was always present" (*ibid* : 47).

Generally, the single women do not prefer to live in rented accommodation on their own. Lack of amenities and conveniences apart, such accommodation does not give them a sense of security. The difficulty of getting cheap and reasonable accommodation poses as a great obstacle in re-establishing themselves after becoming single. The single women are often unable to afford accommodation in a good locality. Discussing the problem of getting cheap accommodation in a safe locality, Mehta notes : "As single women, they did not want to expose themselves to other dangers" (*ibid* : 620). Rented house, of course, offers independence and it is for this advantage that single women sometimes prefer to go in for this type of accommodation. In the sample, 18.2 per cent of the women live in rented accommodation.

A few (7.3 per cent) women live in allotted quarters provided by their employers. Most of them are widows employed on compassionate ground in the same office where their husbands worked. A divorcee or an unmarried woman can hardly expect to get such accommodation.

Of the single women in the sample, 29 per cent are living in hostels. The majority of them are inmates of destitute homes. These women came to be sheltered in the hostels for the destitute under various circumstances. Many of these women live under the shadow of insecurity since they do not know when they would be required to move out. They feel that it is but a temporary shelter. Having no regular means of livelihood, they are totally dependent on the institutions for food and shelter. There are widows, deserted women and unwed mothers among the inmates of destitutes' hostels.

Unwed motherhood is a newly-emergent social problem in the Assamese society. But Assamese society and for that matter, Indian society as a whole does not accept an unwed mother and offer scope for her rehabilitation in society. This has always created untold miseries and problems for a woman with an illegitimate child. The resultant stress from unwed motherhood drives a woman out of her home, her social melieu and even compel her to take a drastic step, e.g., suicide. According to a report of the suicide enquiry committee which studied suicides in Gujarat between 1960-64, one of the causes of high rate of suicide among women was due to illegitimate pregnancies (*Report on the status of women* 1974:99). In some western countries, however, with the social and economic emancipation of women, there is a demand for recognising an unmarried mother and her child as a 'family unit' (Pappu 1975:117). The unwed mothers in the Assamese society literally become outcastes on attainment of such motherhood. Many of them from the rural areas ultimately find their way to the destitutes' hostels in the urban area.

The destitute women hailing from rural areas reflect the changing conditions in the village societies of Assam. Disintegration of the joint family system, weakening of the bonds of kinship and increasing rural poverty have all been to work to create problems for women who become single due to widowhood and broken marriage or remain unmarried for one reason or another, nevertheless, as the study shows, consanguineal kin provide help and co-operation to the single women in many ways. This is so, since in the Assamese society the maintenance of unmarried, divorced or even young widowed daughters is always considered to be the responsibility of the parents.

The Assamese single women try to be economically independent by entering into various occupations available in the urban setting. They are generally concentrated in women-centred occupations in educational institutions, hostels for working women, weaving centres and hospitals. Women employed in offices and industrial units represent a new trend in Assam. A large number (28) of the working women in the sample are engaged in teaching at different levels, from the primary to the post-graduate. According to the *Report on the status of women in India 1974*, this heavy concentration of women in teaching, particularly at the school stage, is because teaching requires relatively little training beyond general education when compared with the requirements of other professions. In the prevailing social conditions, long-term professional training is accessible only to a minority of women belonging to the middle and upper classes. The second reason for women's preference for teaching is the respectability accorded to this profession in society (*ibid* : 206).

The study has indicated that there is a qualitative acceptance of education as a requisite for womenfolk in the contemporary Assamese society. This represents a clear departure from the traditional outlook on the role of women in society as a mere housewife. In the traditional society, education of women was not at all considered important.

For those without enough education, office peon's job and skilled and unskilled jobs provide the avenues for earning a livelihood. In the traditional Assamese Hindu society, there were prejudices against women working in certain occupations. Thus, nursing, sweeping, hair-dressing were taboo for them. But in the new urban setting, caste and other social considerations have significantly weakened in the sphere of occupations. To this extent, a trend towards modernity is visible.

The emergent economic necessities of single women have tended to weaken the traditional role for them of being just housewives and adopt a new role as workers in the altered situation of their lives. It is difficult for a housewife who was always depen-dent on the husband's decision before being single, to re-orient and organise herself in a new role. Adjustment to the new work environment also places additional demands on her. The striking of a balance between the demands of her domestic life and work life is a problem arising out of her single status. She has to simultaneously adjust to the new roles of a working woman, a single parent (when she has a child) and household-level decision-maker. The women who try to meet the traditional role obligations of mother and also spend many hours away from home in paid employment are experiencing a "role overload" or a "double day" (Blumberg and Dwaraki 1980:142). The changed situation and altered circumstances of life compel a single woman to try to stand on her own feet. This in itself may be regarded as a trend towards modernity.

As regards income, it has been found that only about 10 per cent of the single women belong to the high income group. They are employed as college and university teachers, officers, engineers, lawyers and doctors. The majority (52 per cent) of the women in the sample face great hardship due to their poor earnings out of which they have to maintain themselves and their dependents. Moreover, most of the women of lower income group are engaged in purely temporary jobs and usually on contract basis which may be terminated at short notice. They earn their livelihood by weaving, cleaning, sweeping and other petty jobs. They work under considerable stress and anxiety without having any job satisfaction. The single women are often compelled by the circumstances to accept whatever employment comes by their way.

Termination of marriage, either through death of husband or by divorce, along with the necessity of employment affects a woman's familial bonds and other social relations emanating from it. These bonds tend to be considerably weakened in her case. As Kaur notes, the value orientation of Hindu women in general have significantly altered because of change in the family pattern under the impact of urbanization. The constitution of the family, its internal relationship and its outlook towards traditions, superstitions, taboos, etc., have undergone a tremendous change over the years (Kaur 1983:99).

A significant proportion (28.2 per cent) of the women in the sample belong to denuded nuclear families. Most of them are widows. As much as 37.5 per cent of the widows were members of joint households before the death of their respective husbands.

Individualization of earning weakens and breaks up the joint family which is an ideal shelter for widows. As an author points out, it is necessary to assess whether loss of traditional family support mechanisms is beneficial to the status of women or merely leads to greater exploitation (Singh 1980:79). Many single women have to move out of their respective familial melieu in response to their altered circumstances of life. Living on one's own outside family context is a clear indication of social change due to urbanization.

Kinship is an important dimension of social relationship in Assamese society and for that matter, Indian society as a whole. To quote one scholar: "Indians generally tend to live in wide kin networks, though the character of the networks varies according to caste, class and rural-urban residence. These networks provide a sense of belonging, especially to the poor in urban areas who see the world outside them as alien, unhelpful if not hostile" (Srinivas 1981 : 20). The study reveals that as much as 51 per cent of the single women maintain fairly strong ties with their kinsfolk. Kinship continues to be an important dimension of social relationship for the single women. But many women in the sample have much to complain on this aspect of traditional Assamese social organisation. The single women subscribe to the prevailing social values on kinship though many are unable to derive much benefit for themselves out of it. There is thus a significant hiatus between the persistent values and the social reality. While tradition persists in the former, emergent compulsions of urban life have affected the latter.

It is observed that in the cultural context of Assamese society, the single women are in a transitional stage between tradition and modernity. In the religious sphere, they still observe their caste-based norms and customs. But in the changed social situation, some single women are in the process of doing away with the age-old customs. In a study on Indian women, two scholars have made similar observations : "Though basically religious, women today give less importance to temple-going, rituals and superstitions. Orthodox practices have become less significant in the face of progressive urban culture" (Khanna and Varghese 1978 : 203).

In the Indian Hindu society, there are certain rules regarding the dress widows should wear and the nature of their participation in auspicious ceremonies (*Report on the status of women 1974* : 417). The Assamese widows still follow the traditional custom of wearing white dress and shun ornaments. But some educated widows in the urban areas do not any longer observe the restrictions on dress and ornaments. This is a clear indication of changing attitude of educated single women who work for a living.

As regards attitude towards marriage, the majority (63.6 per cent) of the single women favour it and also remarriage of widows and divorcees. Of the 40 widows in the sample, 3 remarried during the period of investigation. Marriage is considered a necessity because of the security, social status and companionship it provides. On the overall attitude of Indian women today towards widow remarriage, Khanna and Varghese note that it is a positive one. It is "... better that a woman should remarry and settle down rather than be at a loose end. She and her children will be better cared for if she remarries and has a proper home" (1978 : 163). Another author observes, on the basis of her sample of study, that widow remarriage was approved by 80 per cent of the employed and 76 per cent of the unemployed women (Devi 1982 : 140).

As the present study has shown, in a sample of 30, only two issueless divorced women remarried during the period of investigation. In most of the cases it is the mother who keeps the children. As one writer appropriately comments, "In our country, to find a mate for a male of any age is still easy, but to find a suitable partner for a divorcee-female is extremely difficult" (Pothen 1987 : 285).

In the context of legal provisions benefitting single women, it is found that they are mostly ignorant of the provisions of law. The study shows that despite the Child Marriage Restraint Act 1929 (amended in 1978), 25 per cent of the single women were married before the age of 15. There are large scale violations of the Child Marriage Restraint Act particularly in the rural areas of India (*Report on the status of women in India* 1974 : 360).

In a study of the divorced Hindu women in the context of legislation, a researcher observes : "The majority of the women were only vaguely aware of the new legislations passed in their favour. They were also not fully aware of the advantages, nor was their knowledge such that they could assess the benefits" (Mehta 1975 : 61). In the present study, only 23.3 per cent of respondents in the sample of divorced or separated women have been benefited from the legal provisions. They happen to be educated and are aware of the provisions of law. As regards succession, most single women display a reluctance to move the court for getting shares of the property to which they are entitled. Lack of funds to file a suit, absence of support from kin and a sense of uneasiness about going publiic on such a matter debar a woman from exercising her legal rights. In Mehta's study also, the "... inhibiting factors against their taking legal action were first the shame attached to admitting publicly that a marriage had failed. Secondly, the money involved in hiring a lawyer" (*ibid.*). However, if funds and support were forthcoming, most of the single women would like to assert their legal rights. There is thus an indication of changing attitude among these women.

The study leads one to surmise that education and separate means of livelihood contribute to the growth of a sense of independence among single women in the Assamese society. These have no doubt helped them to accept the challanges and realities arising out of the single status. But at the same time they are still substantially dependent on the support of close kinsfolk. Kinship provides, though rather loosely, some security and a sense of belonging in the social schema. Commenting on the changing position of Indian women, Srinivas (1981 : 28) notes that what is impressive is the successful blending of traditionalism and modernity in Indian social life and culture. In the context of single women in Assamese society too, there is a mix of tradition and modernity. The single women are in a somewhat diffuse transitional stage, neither wholly traditional nor fully modern.

To provide social recognition, dignity, honour and security to the single women in their life full of many hurdles, due awareness must be created and action plans must be initiated in society. As time moves on, the number of single working women in our society is likely to increase. The need of the hour, therefore, is to take a fresh look at these women, not merely as the representatives of the fair sex whose place is in the home as mere housewives protectively shielded by parents, siblings and husbands, but as persons who have a right to live on their own. To achieve the stated ends, the following concrete actions seem appropriate : (i) preference in employment, (ii) secure accommodation, (iii) provision of creche for working mothers with very young children, (iv) free legal aid through social welfare agencies, (v) social security benefit for single women without employment, and financial and educational support for their children.

APPENDICES

Appendix I

List of Establishments in Guwahati showing women employees and their marital status

Name of the establishments	Marital status: Married	Unmarried	Widow	Divorced/ Separated	Total
(1)	(2)	(3)	(4)	(5)	(6)
Educational :					
1. L.P. School Teachers	210	19	5	3	237
2. M.E. School Teachers	21	6	5	2	34
3. Khanapara Old Govt. Basic School	3	1	-	-	4
4. Dispur Old Govt Basic School	2	1	1	-	4
5. T.C.G.H.S. School	42	5	6	2	55
6. Cotton Collegiate H.S. School	13	1	1	1	16
7. St. Mary's English High School	10	1	1	-	12
8. Gopal Boro H.S. School	9	1	-	-	10
9. Panbazar Girls' High School	27	7	-	-	34
10. Kamakhya High School	3	1	-	-	4
11. Bhaskar Bidyapith School	4	1	1	-	6
12. Arya Bidyapith School	2	1	1	-	4

(1)	(2)	(3)	(4)	(5)	(6)
13. North-Guwahati Girls' High School	10	2	-	-	12
14. Rangmahal High School	3	1	-	-	4
15. Kaliram Baruah Girls' High School	12	2	2	-	16
16. Azara Higher Secondary School	5	3	-	-	8
17. Natun Fatasil High School	1	1	-	-	2
18. Sri Aurobinda Vidya Mandir High School	2	1	-	-	3
19. Pub-Guwahati High School	5	1	-	-	6
20. Ulubari High School	3	-	1	-	4
21. Gauhati University Model High School	7	-	2	-	9
22. P.S. Dhanuka Bidyalaya, Dedar Road	5	3	1	-	9
23. Cotton College	23	7	-	3	33
24. Handique Girls' College	28	7	3	1	39
25. B. Baruah College	20	2	-	-	22
26. Arya Bidyapith College	11	4	-	-	15
27. Pragjyotish College	13	3	-	-	16
28. North-Guwahati College	2	1	-	-	3

(1)	(2)	(3)	(4)	(5)	(6)
29. Assam Engineering College	2	1	-	1	4
30. Gauhati University	25	6	2	1	34
Official establishment :					
31. N.F. Railway, Maligaon Head Office	61	35	7	-	103
32. Janata Bhawan, Dispur	3	1	1	-	5
33 (a) Public Work Deptt., Dispur	8	1	-	-	9
(b) Finance Deptt., Dispur	9	2	1	-	12
34. Secretariat, Dispur	22	6	3	1	32
35. Assembly, Dispur	2	1	1	-	4
36. Assam Khadi Village Industry Board	1	5	-	-	6
37. Girls' Polytechnic Office staff	-	1	1	-	2
38. Gauhati Municipal Corpn.	20	11	-	-	31
39. All India Radio	11	1	3	-	15
40. Gauhati Refinery Noonmati	9	6	7	-	22
41. Office of the Chief Engineer, P.W.D., Building Wing	13	9	1	-	23
42. P.W.D. Road Wing	19	7	2	-	28
43. Gauhati High Court	6	7	4	-	17

(1)	(2)	(3)	(4)	(5)	(6)
44. Bar Council, Gauhati	10	7	1	-	18
45. Post & Telegraph Deptt.	8	7	3	1	19
46. Assam State co-operative Marketing & Consumers Federation Ltd., Guwahati	6	2	-	-	8
47. Office of the Chief Engineer, A.S.E.B., Ulubari	2	3	-	1	6
48. Deptt. of Fishery	7	2	-	-	9
49. Directorate of Economics & Statistics Assam	13	5	-	-	18
50. Inspector General of Prisons	-	1	-	-	1
51. Office of the C.P.W.D.	5	3	2	-	10
52. Publication Board, Assam	3	3	-	-	6
53. Deptt. of Veterinary	36	10	2	-	48
54. F.C.I., Ulubari	5	4	-	-	9
55. North Eastern Handicraft, Bamunimaidan	3	3	-	-	6
56. Assam Industrial Development Corpn.	1	4	-	-	5
57. Gauhati University Library	3	-	2	-	5
58. L.I. Corporation	6	1	-	-	7

(1)	(2)	(3)	(4)	(5)	(6)
59. Office of the Registrar, Gauhati University	3	-	2	-	5
60. Office of the Publicity	3	1	-	-	4
61. Deptt. of Police	5	7	-	-	12
62. Assam State Housing Board	5	3	-	-	8
63. Assam Seed Corpn.	4	1	-	-	5
64. Small Industry Extenstion	3	1	-	-	4
Training Institute :					
65. Public Health Laboratory	5	4	-	-	9
66. Assam Express	4	8	-	1	13
67. Himalayan Printers	1	1	-	-	2
68. Public Health Service, Dispur	6	-	1	-	7
69. Department of Social Welfare	2	3	-	1	6
70. Text Book Production	4	2	-	-	6
71. S.S.I.D.C. Industrial Estate	4	1	1	-	6
72. Hindustan Polythene	2	4	2	3	11
Banking :					
73. Apex Bank, Panbazar	1	2	3	-	6
74. Reserve Bank of India	5	6	-	-	11
75. State Bank of India	2	4	1	-	7
76. S.B.I. Regional Office, Bhangagarh	-	3	-	-	3

(1)	(2)	(3)	(4)	(5)	(6)
77. S.B.I., New Guwahati	4	2	2	-	8
78. S.B.I. West Guwahati	2	-	-	-	2
79. S.B.I. Regional Head Office, Bharalumukh	4	9	-	-	13
80. S.B.I. Regional Recruitment Board	1	5	-	-	6
81. Purbanchal Bank, Silpukhuri	2	1	-	-	3
82. United Commercial Bank Ltd., Fancy Bazar	2	5	-	-	7
Female Occupational Centres :					
83. State Home for Women.					
(a) Inmates	-	43	12	2	57
(b) Office staff	8	4	1	2	15
84. Weaving Centre Industrial Estate	1	14	-	4	19
85. Power loom Production Centre, Industrial Estate	10	4	2	2	18
86. Assam Polythene Industrial Estate	-	2	4	-	6
87. Assam Sericulture & Weaving Deptt.	8	9	3	1	21
88. Red Cross Nursing Staff	-	32	-	-	32
89. Dispur Polyclinic	-	7	-	-	7
90. (a) G.M.C. Nursing staff and Doctor	18	25	2	-	45

(1)	(2)	(3)	(4)	(5)	(6)
(b) G.M.C. Nursing Sister	12	2	-	1	15
(c) G.M.C. Staff Nurses	27	23	-	-	50
91. Kalapahar Nursing Home	2	8	1	4	15
92. Railway Hospital Nursing staff	9	1	-	-	10
93. Gandhibasti Working Women's Hostel	-	20	1	0	21
94. Narengi Working Women's Hostel	3	35	3	6	47
95. (a) Kasturba Ashram	-	9	2	-	11
(b) Other	-	-	3	2	5
	987	549	119	46	1701

Appendix II

Ms. Jeuti Barooah, M.Sc.; L.L.B.
Research Scholar
Add : Research Officer,
Law Research Institute, Guahati High Court.

Topic of Research : Single women in contemporary Assamese Hindu Society.

Dear Sir/Madam

May I ask your assistant in this research by filling up the following table with the names of the lady employees of your esteemed institution. The list requires only the names of Assamese Hindu Women.

Thanking you,

Sincerely yours,

(J. Barooah)

Name & Address of the Institution :

....

....

Sl. No.	Names of the Lady Employees	Approx. age	Marital status (married, unmarried, widow, divorcee, separted)	Occupational status	
				Designation	monthly income

Appendix III

Age distribution of the universe

Age Group	Total	MARITAL STATUS							
		Married		Married		Widow		Divorcee or Separated	
		No.	%	No.	%	No.	%	No.	%
15-19	22	-	-	21	95.45	-	-	1	4.55
20-24	188	26	13.83	156	82.98	4	2.12	2	1.06
25-29	301	155	51.49	136	45.18	5	1.66	5	1.66
30-34	282	190	67.37	70	24.82	11	3.90	11	3.90
35-39	218	139	63.76	43	19.72	25	11.46	11	5.04
40-44	115	78	67.83	14	12.17	19	16.52	4	3.47
45-49	95	54	56.84	15	15.78	22	23.16	4	4.21
50-54	44	25	56.82	5	11.36	9	20.45	5	11.36
55-59	18	8	44.44	5	27.77	5	27.77	-	-
60 & above	5	-	-	3	60%	2	40%	-	-
Age not stated	413	312	75.54	81	19.61	17	4.11	3	0.73
	1701	987		549		119		46	

Appendix IV

SCHEDULE NO. 1 : GENERAL

Name :

1. Educational qualification with specified subject :
2. Year of passing the High School Leaving Certificate examintion :
3. Place of birth : District :

   Town/Village :
4. Father's occupation :
5. Brief description of father's property :
6. Where did you spend your
   (a) Early childhood :
   (b) Schooling years :
   (c) College years :
   (d) After College :
   (e) Living in Guwahati since :
7. With whom you are staying now ?
8. Number of your family members and their relation with you :
9. Occupational history :

Sl. No.	Name of Occupation	Year	Place	Remark

10. Circumstances & Reasons for taking up employment :

11. Do you have any self-acquired property (including L.I.C., bank balance, land, houses, etc.) ?

12. Number of cinemas seen in the last month :

13. What are the journals and magazines you subscribe :

14. Name your favourite book and the author :

15. What are your hobbies ? :

16. Are you a member of any social institution? :

SCHEDULE NO. 2 : FOR DIVORCEE/WIDOW

1. Date of marriage :

2. Age at marriage :

3. Husband's age at marriage :

4. Duration of married life :

5. What were you doing at the time of your marriage— studying or working ? :

6. Husband's occupation :

7. Number of issues born and their ages : (a) son
   (b) daughter :

8. Husband's property :
   (a) movable :
   (b) immovable :

9. Have you got anything out of your husband's property? :

10. Are you deprived from getting any property for which you are entitled to? :

    If yes, do you want to file any suit? :

    If not, give reasons :

GLOSSARY

Abiyoi :	Unmarried woman
Adhi :	(Share-cropping) A special contract by which a person cultivates the land of another person on condition of delivering a share of the produce.
Ai-nam :	Songs addressed to presiding deity of pox.
Amabashya :	The day of the conjunction of the sun and moon.
Ambubashi :	Four days in the month of Assarh (June-July) when the earth is supposed to be unclean.
Annaprasana	Ceremonial giving of first rice meal to infants.
Api-oja :	*Api*-girl; *oja*-lead singer ; an institution of singing and dancing.
Bamun :	Brahmin
Bhada :	August-September
Bihu :	The day on which the sun enters the sign, *Libra* or *Capricornus*. The Assamese observe these as festive days.
Bihuwan :	Ceremonial Bihu gift
Biya-nam :	Marriage songs
Bohag :	April-May
Chadar :	A wrap draping the loins over the *mekhela* and also the upper part of the body, used by a woman.
Dhai-nam :	Songs relating to birth and delivery.
Dhenki :	Wooden husking lever plied by feet.
Dhoti :	White loin cloth worn by men.
Ekadashi :	The eleventh day of the lunar half of the month.

Endi : Cloth obtained from a species of silk worm which feeds on castor leaves.

Gamocha : Hand-woven towel

Gosai-ghar : Prayer room

Hat : Market place

Kabacha : Life-saving garment

Kumari-worship : Virgin worship

Laroo : A ball of confection.

Mahari : Account-keeper

Masur-dal : Lentil

Mekhela : Women's dress : cloth to cover the lower part of the body from waist down to the ankles.

Mel : A gethering of elders of a locality or village to decide on a dispute.

Mitir- kutumb : Two categories of kin; i.e., affines and agnates.

Muga : A silk yarn of golden hue.

Nam : Prayer-songs

Namghar : Prayer house

Nam-kirttan : Devotional song

Nisukani-git : Lullaby

Pat : A kind of silk (mulberry) produced in Assam.

Patibrata : A woman devoted to husband

Pitha : Sweet meat; cake

Prasad : Food offered to the deity.

Purnima : The day of the full moon.

Purohit : Priest

Riha : A piece of feminine garment to cover the upper part of the body.

Rongali Bihu : Bhu observed during mid-April; onset of Assamese New Year.

Sampradan :	Giving away (of bride)
Santi-biya :	Purifying marriage after a girl's first menstruation before joining her husband.
Satra :	A vaishnavite religious institution in Assam.
Satradhikar :	Head of *satra* institution.
Sraddha :	Funeral rites at the end of death pollution period.
Sudir :	Non-Brahmin, Sudra
Thapana :	Altar
Ural :	Wooden mortar
Uruka :	The eve of *Magh* (January-February) Bihu.

REFERENCES

Acharyya, N.N.1987. *A Brief History of Assam,* Omsons Publications, New Delhi.

Altekar, A.S. 1938. *The position of women in Hindu civilization* (Reprinted 1978), Motilal Banarsidass, Delhi.

Bar-Barua, Hiteswar 1981. *Ahomar Din* (Assamese), Assam Publication Board, Guwahati.

Bardoloi, N. 1983. *Asamar Loka Sanskriti* (Assamese), Published by Bina Library, Guwahati.

Barua, B.K. 1959. 'Assamese language and early Assamese literature', *Aspects of the Heritage of Assam* (ed. by K.N. Dutta), Indian History Congress, 22nd session, Gauhati : 56-69.

. . . . 1969. *Cultural History of Assam,* Vol. I. LBS Publication.

Barua, G.R. 1884. *Assam Buranji* (Reprinted 1972; Assamese), Publication Board, Assam.

Barua, Hemchandra 1900. *Hema-Kosha,* The Assamese English Dictionary (ed. by D. Barua, 1978). Hemchandra Library, Gauhati.

Barua, Induprava 1975. 'Asamat mahila jagaran aru mahila samitir bhumika', *Smaranika* (ed. by I. Miri; Assamese), Souvenir, International women's year, Gauhati : 22-31.

Bhagabati, A.C. 1988. 'Tribal transformation in Assam and North-East India : An appraisal of emerging ideological dimensions': Presidential Address, *Seventififth Indian Science Congress,* Indian Science Congress Association, Calcutta :1-26.

Bharali, Sailen 1984. *Asamiya Loka-natya Parampara* (Assamese), Bani Prakash, Pathsala, Assam.

Bhattacharyya, B.K. (ed.) 1988 *Problems of Urban Development in Guwahati,* Omsons Publications, New Delhi.

Bhuyan, A.C. (et al. eds.) 1978. *Political History of Assam,* Vol. II, Government of Assam.

Bhuyan, S.K. 1965. 'Noble Women of Assam', *Studies in the History of Assam,* published by Smti. L. Bhuyan, Gauhati, Assam : 71 - 73.

Blumberg, R.L. & Dwaraki, L. 1980. *India's educated women : Options and Constraints,* Hindustan Publishing Corporation, Delhi.

Cantlie, Audrey. 1984. *The Assamese,* London studies on South Asia, No. 3. Curzon Press Ltd. London and Dublin.

Chatterji, S.K. 1959. 'Assam and India', *Aspects of the Heritage of Assam* (ed. by K.N. Dutta), Indian History Congress, 22nd session, Gauhati : 1-7.

Choudhury, P.C. 1957. *The history of civilization of the people of Assam to the twelfth century A.D.* (Revised edition 1987), Spectrum Publications, Guwahati.

Das, B.M. 1987. *The Peoples of Assam,* Gian Publishing House, Delhi.

Datta, B.N. 1980. 'The Assamese folk-mind', *Assam and the Assamese mind,* Assam Sahitya Sabha, Jorhat.

.... 1981. 'The Tribal and the Non-tribal in the context of Assamese society and culture', *The Journal of the North-East India Council For Social Science Research,* Vol. V No. II, October :8-12.

Desai, S.T. 1912. *Mulla Principles of Hindu Law* (Reprinted 1986), N.M. Tripathi Pvt. Ltd., Bombay.

Dev, B.J. & Lahiri, D.K. 1984. *Cosmogeny of caste and social mobility in Assam.* Mittal Publications, Delhi.

Devi, U.L. 1982. *Status and Employment of Women in India,* B.R. Publishing Corporation, Delhi.

Dutta, Hem 1975. *The Nineteen Forty Two Upheaval in Assam,* Praghyoti Prakashan, Jorhat-1, Assam.

Gait, Edward 1905. *A History of Assam* (Reprinted 1984) LBS Publications Gauhati, Assam.

Geddie, William (ed.) 1971. *Chambers's Twentieth Century Dictionary* (Sixth impression), Allied Publishers, New Delhi.

Gogoi, Padmeswar 1968. *The Tai and the Tai Kingdoms.* Department of Publication, Gauhati University.

Hate, Chanrakala 1969. *Changing status of women,* Allied Publishers, Bombay.

Herskovits, M.J. 1947. *Cultural Anthropology* (Reprinted 1958), Oxford & IBH Publishing Co., Delhi.

Jain, Devaki (ed.) 1975. *Indian women*, Publications Division, Ministry of Information and Broadcasting, Government of India.

Kakati, B.K. 1941. *Assamese, Its formation and Development* (Revised edition 1987), LBS Publication, Gauhati.

Kapadia, K.M. 1955. *Marriage and Family in India* (Reprinted 1988), Oxford University Press, Calcutta.

Kapur, Promilla 1970. *Marriage and the working woman in India*, Vikas Publication, Delhi.

..... 1974. *The changing status of the working woman in India*, Vikas Publications, Delhi.

..... 1978. *The life and world of call-girls in India*, Vikas Publications, Delhi.

Kaur, Inderjeet 1983. *Status of Hindu women in India*, Chugh Publication, Allahabad.

Kaushik, Susheela (ed) 1985. *Women in society : Women's oppression: Patterns and Perspectives*, Shakti Books, New Delhi.

Khanna, G. & Varghese, M.A. 1978. *Indian Women Today*, Vikas Publishing House, Delhi.

Kuppuswamy, B. 1972. *Social change in India* (Reprinted 1977), Vikas Publishing House, Delhi.

Lahkar, Bina 1987. *Development in Women Education* (Study of Assam), Omsons Publications, Delhi.

Lowie, R.H. 1950. *Social Organization* (Reprinted 1966), Routledge & Kegan Paul Ltd., London.

M'Cosh, John 1837. *Topography of Assam* (Reprinted 1975), Sanskaran Prakashak, Delhi.

Mehta, Rama 1975. *Divorced Hindu Woman*, Vikas Publishing House, Delhi.

Minattur, Joseph 1980. 'Women and the Law : Constitutional Rights and Continuing Inequalities', *Women in Contemporary India and South Asia* (ed. by Alfred de Souza), Monohar Publications, Delhi : 165-178.

Miri, Indira (ed.) 1975. *Smaranika*, Souvenir, International women's year, Gauhati.

Misra, Tilottama 1987. *Literature and society in Assam,* Omsons Publications, Delhi.

Nath, D.P. 1988. 'Master Plan for Guwahati and its Implementation', *Problems of Urban Development in Guwahati* (ed. by B.K. Bhattacharyya), Omsons Publications, New Delhi.

Neog, Maheswar 1959. 'The Vaisnava Renaissance in Assam', *Aspects of the Heritage of Assam* (ed. by K.N. Dutta), Indian History Congress, 22nd session, Gauhati : 31-49.

Neog, Maheswar 1969. ' Tradition of classical Music and Dance', *Assam* (ed. by S. Barkataki), National Book Trust, New Delhi.

..... (Compiled) 1983. *Orunodoi* 1846-54, Publication Board, Assam.

Pappu, Shyamala 1975. 'Legal provisions — An Assessment', *Indian Women* (ed. by D. Jain), Publications Divisions, Government of India :113-24.

Pothen, S. 1987. *Divorce, Its causes and consequences in Hindu society,* Shakti Books, Delhi.

Prabhu, P.H. 1963. *Hindu Social Organization,* fourth edn., Popular Prakashan, Bombay.

Rao, N.J. Usha 1983. *Women in a developing society,* Ashish Publishing House, New Delhi.

Robinson, W. 1841. *A Descriptive Account of Assam* (Reprinted 1975), London.

Saikia, N. (Compiled) 1984. *Assam-Bandhu,* Publication Board, Assam.

Sarma, S.N. 1959. 'The Satra Institution of Assam', *Aspects of the Heritage of Assam* (ed. by K.N. Dutta), Indian History Congress, 22nd session, Gauhati : 50-55.

..... 1981. 'Social changes in Assam 1750-1950' *Journal of the University of Gauhati* (M. Neog et al. eds.), Vol. XXVIII-XXIX No. 1 : 109-121.

Singh, A.M. 1980. 'The Study of Women in South-Asia : Some Current Methodological and Research Issues', *Women in Contemporary India and South Asia* (ed. by Alfred de Souza), Monohar Publications, New Delhi : 61-93.

Souza, Alfred de (ed) 1980. 'An Introduction', *Women in Contem-*

porary India and South Asia, Monohar Publications, New Delhi: 1-29.

Srinivas, M.N. 1978. *The changing position of Indian women* (second impression 1981), Oxford University Press, Delhi.

Reports and Journals :

All India Reporter manual, 1979.

Assam Information, 1983.

Census of India 1971 :

Series 3, Part II-C (ii),

.... Part VI-B; Special Survey reports on selected towns — Gauhati,

.... Part IX.

Census of India, 1981 :

Series 1, Part II B (i); Primary Census Abstract,

General Population,

Series 3, Part X-A; Assam : Town Directory.

Child Marriage Restraint Act, 1929, amended in 1978.

Current Indian Statutes, 1978.

MAPS AND FIGURES

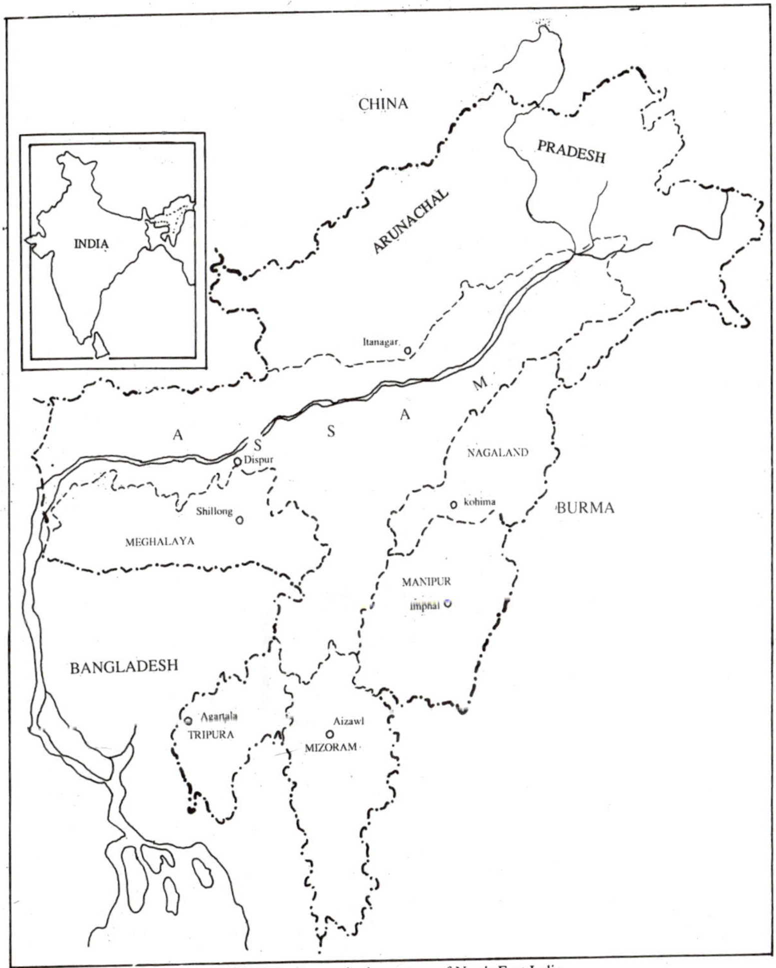

FIGURE 2. Assam in the context of North-East India

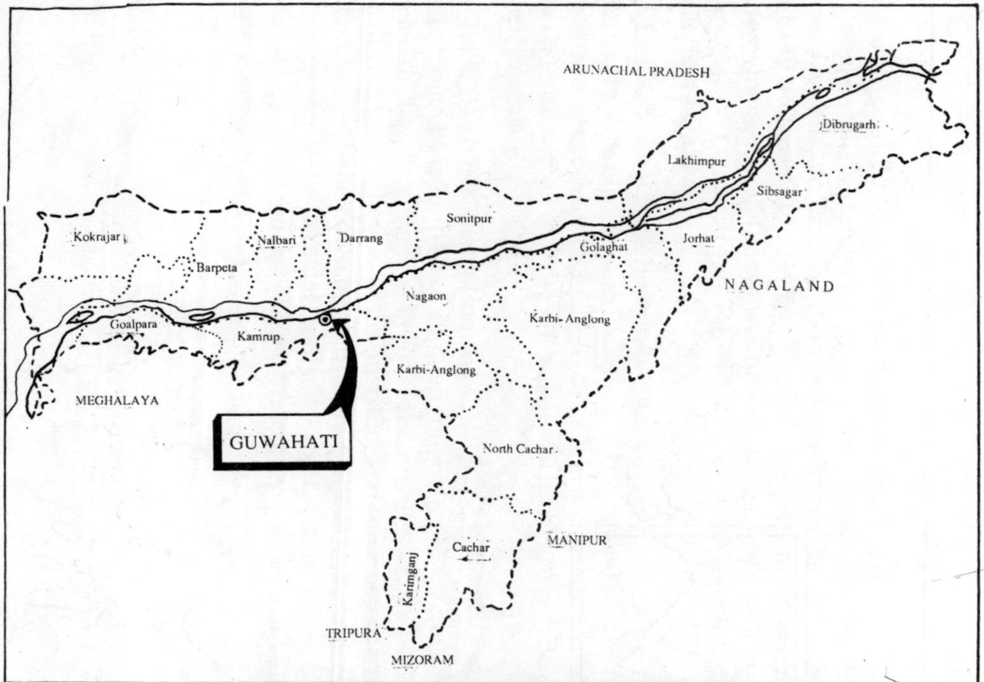

FIGURE 3. Assam, showing the different districts and the place of field work.

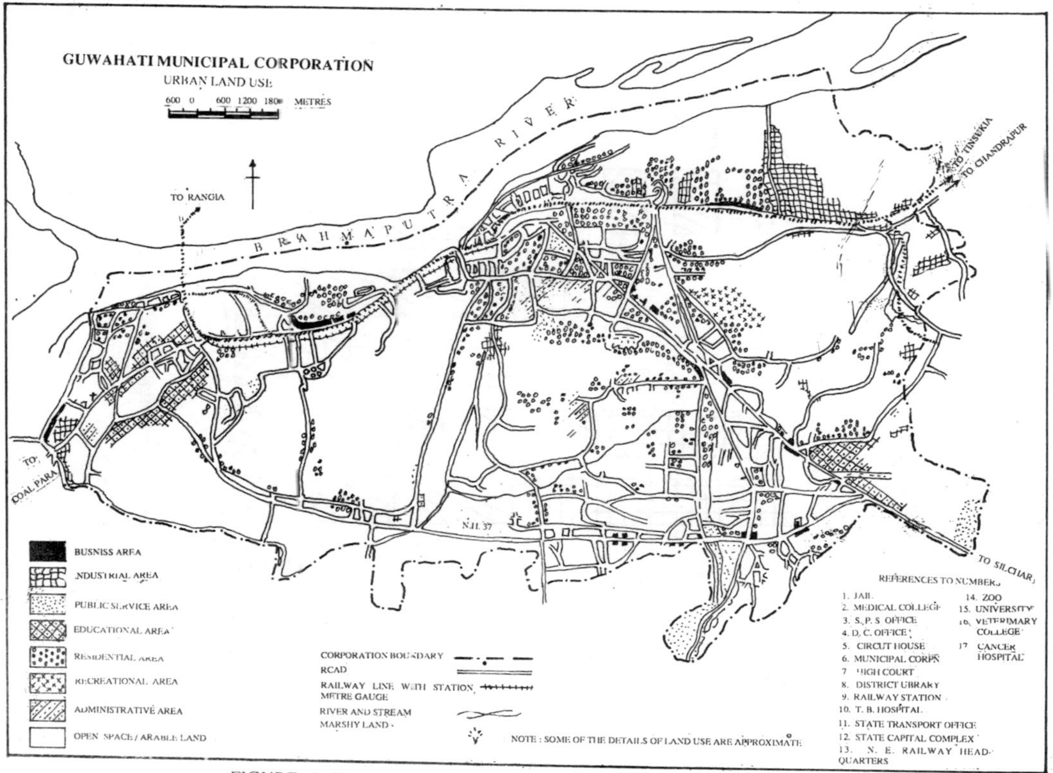

FIGURE 4. The urban area of Guwahati Source : Census of India 1981 series– 3, Assam part–x–A

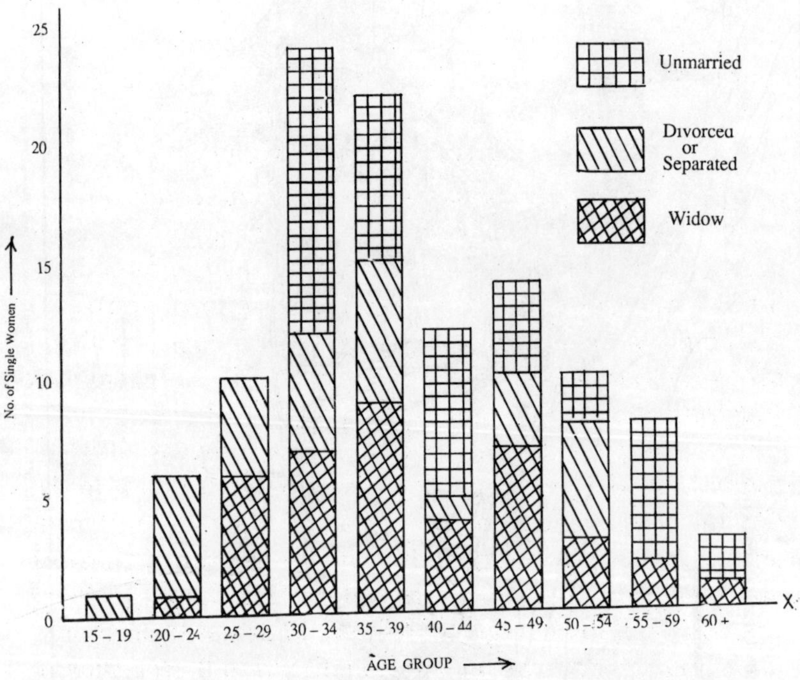

FIGURE 5. AGE DISTRIBUTION OF SINGLE WOMEN

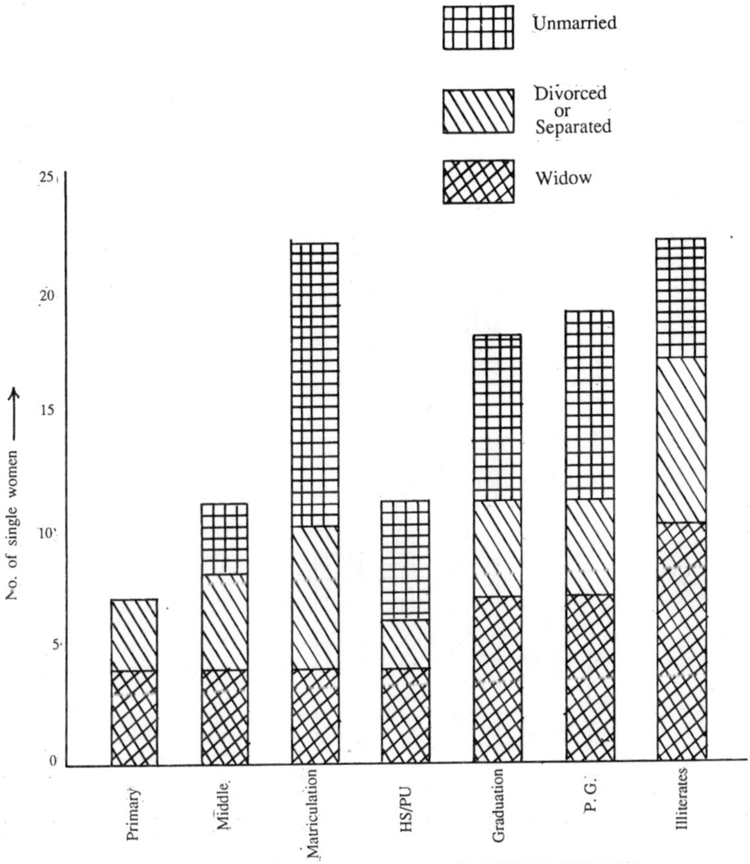

FIGURE 6. EDUCATIONAL LEVEL OF SINGLE WOMEN

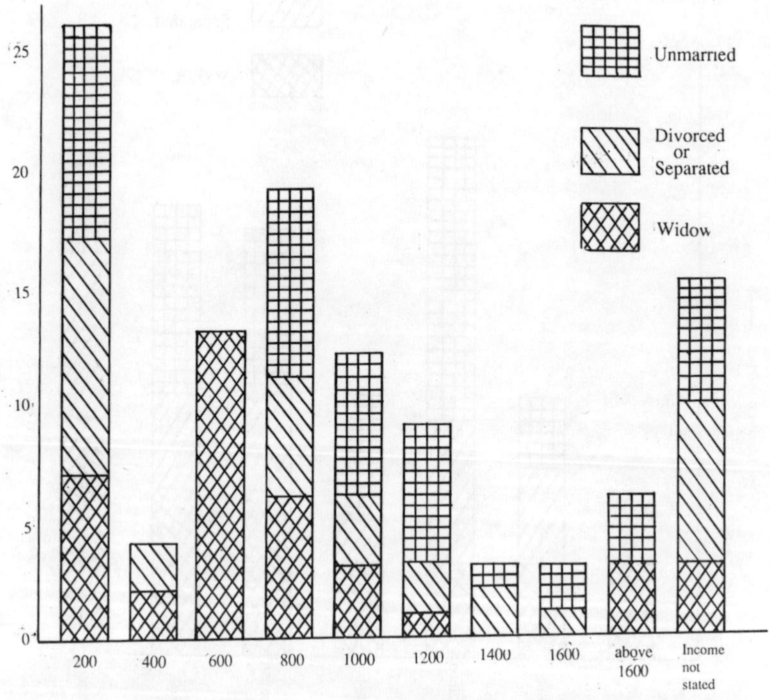

FIGURE 7. INCOME LEVEL OF SINGLE WOMEN

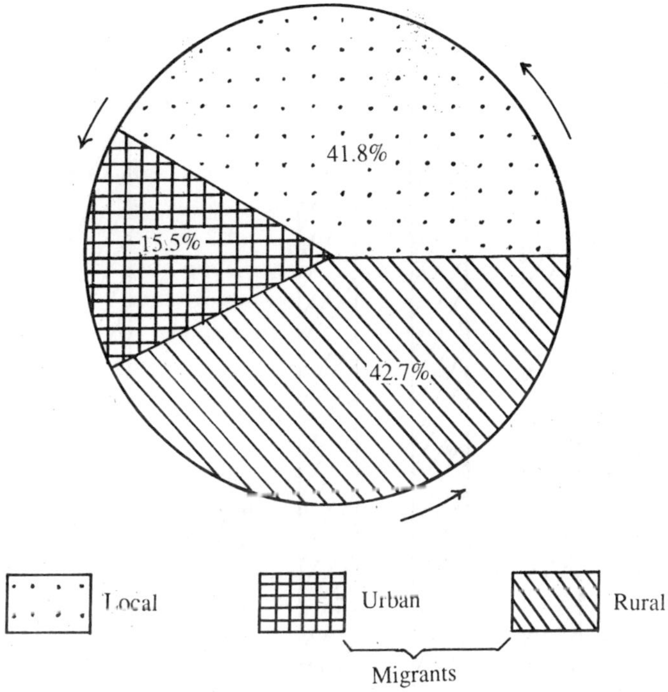

FIGURE 8. Pattern of migration of single women to the city

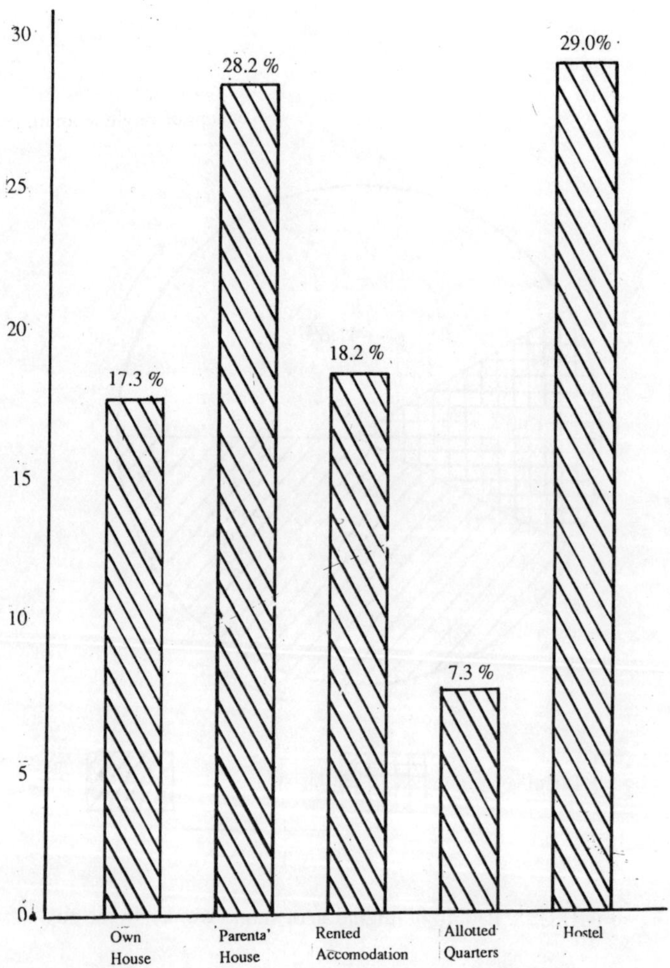

FIGURE 9. LIVING ARRANGEMENTS OF SINGLE WOMEN

INDEX

Y